I0048949

Sisyphus in Management

Stefan Kühl is professor of sociology at the University of Bielefeld in Germany and works as a consultant for Metaplan, a consulting firm based in Princeton, Hamburg, Shanghai, Singapore, Versailles and Zurich. He studied sociology and history at the University of Bielefeld (Germany), Johns Hopkins University in Baltimore (USA), Université Paris-X-Nanterre (France) and the University of Oxford (UK).

Other Books by Stefan Kühl

Organizations: A Systems Approach
(Routledge 2013)
Ordinary Organizations: Why Normal Men Carried Out the Holocaust
(Polity Press 2016)
When the Monkeys Run the Zoo: The Pitfalls of Flat Hierarchies
(Organizational Dialogue Press 2017)
The Rainmaker Effect: Contradictions of the Learning Organization
(Organizational Dialogue Press 2018)

To contact us:

Metaplan
Goethestraße 16
D-25451 Quickborn
Germany
Phone: +49 41 06 61 70
info@organizationaldialoguepress.com
www.metaplan.com

Stefan Kühl

Sisyphus in Management

The Futile Search for the Optimal Organizational Structure

Organizational Dialogue Press
Princeton, Hamburg, Shanghai, Singapore, Versailles, Zurich

ISBN (Print) 978-1-7349619-0-4
ISBN (EPUB) 978-1-7349619-1-1

Copyright © 2020 by Stefan Kühl

All rights reserved. No part of this publication may be reproduced or transmitted in any form or by any means, without permission in writing from the author.

Translated by: Philip Schmitz
Cover Design: Guido Klütsch
Typesetting: Thomas Auer
Project Management: Tabea Koepp
www.organizationaldialoguepress.com

Contents

.

Foreword:
Optimal Organizational Structure and the Search for the Organizational Holy Grail

A general notion of what an organization actually is formed in the 17th and 18th centuries, and the dream of an optimal organizational structure existed well before then. Even the Sassanids who dominated Persia in the third century CE debated ways to optimize the manufacturing of glass and silk. In the late Middle Ages and Early Modern Age, at the height of the Venetian city state, counselors discussed how to organize shipbuilding most efficiently. The Dutch and British merchants who dispatched their ships to Asia to buy spices in the 16th and 17th centuries, debated the best way to structure their ventures. And today, corporations, public administrations, the military, hospitals, universities, schools, and associations spend a great amount of time identifying the form of organization that offers them the framework best suited for the optimal performance of their work.

But do such optimal organizational structures really exist? Granted, management books, articles in economics journals, and the downpour of slides presented in lectures for practitioners suggest that the organizational Holy Grail has been found—or at least that its discovery is near at hand. Yet on closer examination, it becomes obvious how much contradiction organizations must contend with as they strive for perfection.

On the one side, employees are supposed to compete with one another within the organization as "entrepreneurs within the company," while on the other they are supposed to cooperate with their coworkers. The motto is: we are all pulling together, but only the best will prevail. In one sense, there is the demand that employees follow their own path, yet at the same time they must not lose sight of the organization's overall goal. Again, the motto: everybody finds their own way of doing things, but we are still in the same boat. On the one hand, employees are supposed to break the rules that have been handed down from above—if necessary—while on the other they must respect the structures the organization has put in place. The motto is: do what you like, but don't break any of the written or unwritten laws. On the one hand, there needs to be enough room for flexible, creative lateral thinkers to maneuver, while still using the organization's resources as effectively as possible. The motto here is: be unorthodox, just don't interfere with the standardization process which is taking place in the name of efficiency.

Particularly in organizations that decentralize decision-making competencies, reduce the levels of their hierarchies, and eliminate strict boundaries between departments, fundamental coordination problems emerge. How does one arrange coordination between units that are independent and primarily self-referencing? How can one organize cooperation between partially autonomous groups, process lines, sectors, or profit centers even though they are permitted a high degree of autonomy? How does one find a balance between the required and the encouraged local rationality of teams as opposed to the organization's overall rationale? The basic problem organizations face is this: the more individual units are in a position to gain independence, the more urgent but also the more complicated it becomes to integrate them into the organization as a whole. As differentiation into self-organized, partially autonomous units increases, integration becomes more difficult and simultaneously also more necessary.

Under these conditions, the search for an optimal organizational structure resembles the efforts of Sisyphus who tries in vain to reach the top of the hill with his boulder. Just as the boulder rolls away from him time and time again, managers' hopes of finding the optimal organizational structure are repeatedly dashed. Measures intended to streamline organizational design produce undesired side effects that frequently emerge only after some time. While a central organizational problem may be brought under control, it is at the cost of new areas that present themselves to management and call for improvement.

For companies, public administrations, hospitals, universities, or the military, this book destroys the hope of being able to find an optimal organizational structure. It explains the undesired side effects and the paradoxical outcomes that management battles as it strives for perfection and quality. Following a basic discussion of the problems entailed by the search for the optimal organizational structure in Chapter 1—which can easily be read at the end—I turn to the central questions that management poses when it attempts to optimize an organization. Why do employees resist their own "empowerment" within the framework of decentralization measures (Chapter 2)? Why can organizations be structured like a big internal market (Chapter 3)? Why does quality management often result in more bureaucracy instead of greater quality (Chapter 4)? Why does systematic decentralization in some cases result in a centralization of decision-making (Chapter 5)? Why do group work projects, according to the criteria of their promoters, succeed to a limited degree and then ultimately turn out to be projects that have "failed successfully" (Chapter 6)? How do businesses attempt to orient themselves according to "good management" concepts and then try, this best practice orientation notwithstanding, to present themselves as "unique" (Chapter 7)? And how should they manage the difficulties encountered in searching for the optimal organizational structure (Chapter 8)?

The Three Aspects of an Organization

When analyzing organizations, the important thing is always to bear in mind that there are three aspects to an organization: the *display side*, which is to say, the embellished façade that is shown to the outside world; the *formal side*, consisting of the more or less precisely synchronized expectations members must meet if they wish to retain membership; and the *informal side*, the routines that have crept into day-to-day operations and have formed in the shadow of the formal aspect.

It is an unavoidable outcome of the division of labor that the members of an organization focus on one particular aspect (Kühl 2013, 89).

Middle management is dominated by specialists in the formal programming of organizations. This is where targets are conceived, and new rules formulated which the employees must observe. The formal targets must then be implemented in the organization's operative areas, although construing, reinterpreting, and dodging the formalized requirements often takes a good amount of playful creativity. Understandably, those who specialize in the informal side of things are not flagged on the organizational chart, for example, as a "Chief Informality Officer." Often it is the employees in human resources development or the training and education department who assume the role of contacts for everything that isn't readily subsumed under the organization's formal structure. One of the major responsibilities of those who hold the top positions is to dress up the organization's display side—with assistance from their communications, press, and marketing departments.

It may be considered good style for members of an organization to emphasize that they always keep an eye on all three aspects; depending on their position they tend to see one of the three in terms of an absolute. The experts in formal structure frequently view the organization's widely diverse forms of informality and the everyday infractions of the rules from one perspective only: this has to be "fixed." They call in quality management consultants who are charged with identifying the frequent deviations from the rules and eliminating them. Comprehensive organizational management software is purchased as a means of making technical provisions against deviations from standards. Or, specific departments are set up to control processes or ensure conformity—currently known as "compliance"—thereby keeping deviations from the rules to a minimum. Finally, there are the organizational culture experts who often view the informal work processes as both a bastion of humaneness in an alienated work environment and the key to increased profitability. Improving the organization's "chemistry" is seen as a launching point for creating happier employees as well as increasing the bottom line. Meanwhile, at the highest management echelons, one can observe a preference for viewing an organization's internal processes from the perspective of its display side. As early as

1938, Chester Barnard (Barnard 1938, 120), who was a senior executive at telecommunications company AT&T for a time, noted that high level managers frequently cannot keep track of their own organization's rules and regulations and are to no small degree clueless as to the factors, attitudes, and behaviors that shape the organization from day to day. Specializing and focusing on one particular aspect of an organization makes sense in terms of the division of labor. Just as it makes sense for companies to employ specialists in the fields of purchasing, production, and sales, or for a hospital to employ separate experts to provide medical care, handle the accounting for services performed, and to clean the halls, it also appears to make functional sense that organizations keep people with different kinds of expertise on hand to manage their formal sides, informal sides, and display sides. A cabinet minister would be demanding too much of herself, not to mention her ministry, if—in addition to functioning as a display window for political decisions—she aspired as well to understanding the relevant formal rules and regulations that applied to the organization and to keeping track of the various informal coordination processes within the ministry. For production line workers in an automotive supply factory, it is enough if they are taught which formal demands apply to them and learn how to circumvent the demands informally if the need should arise. They do not need to feel responsible for building the company's external image.

Nevertheless, if the goal is to gain a comprehensive understanding of the way an organization works, one must be able not only to grasp all three aspects and their respective rationales, but also to understand how those three aspects mesh. As a point of departure for my analysis in this book, I take the display side of an organization that has been spruced up with trendy management topics. I show that organizations do not in any way function according to the principles propagated via their display side. Drawing on a large number of pioneering organizations, I demonstrate how processes function in the shadow of the display side and point out the very significant degree to which their functioning contradicts what is presented to the outside world. Yet this is not intended to challenge the functionality of the display side. On the contrary, if an organization presented itself to the world the way it actually works, its authenticity would presumably quickly lead to its demise.

In my two other books about new forms of organizations—*When the Monkeys Run the Zoo: The Pitfalls of Flat Hierarchies* and *The Rainmaker Effect: Contradictions of the Learning Organization*—I concentrated on showing what would happen if the principles communicated through an organization's display side were implemented on a one-to-one basis. In the present book, I employ an in-depth analysis of pioneering organizations to systematically look behind their display side and show what effects the decentralization and dehierarchization measures undertaken on the formal side have on an organization's informal side.

From the perspective of organizational science, the contradictions, dilemmas, and paradoxes that can be observed when one peers behind the display side do not represent pathology in any sense. Systems-theoretical organizational research contends that there is no way organizations can avoid grappling with contradictory expectations because they are thrust on organizations from the outside. Such contradictory expectations can be cushioned by delegating them to various departments or hierarchical levels, but the inescapable result is that they lead to differences between those departments and hierarchical levels.

Opposing the Urge to Have "the Very Latest Thing"

In management literature, there is a regrettable sense of urgency to be totally up-to-date and have the very latest approach. Perhaps this need for something new is understandable at first glance. Who will be able to introduce the next best practice model is the subject of bitter competition among organizational consultants. In the publishing market, the only way an author of management books can still position a bestseller is to proclaim nothing short of a revolution.

As a rule, the new concepts are merely an attempt to sell old wine in new bottles. The post-bureaucratic forms of organization once referred to as "flexible firms," "modular organizations," or "adhocracies" are now advertised as "agile systems," "fractal organizations" or "holacracy." Considerations on popular networking concepts that were being propagated several years ago as "virtual organizations" or "network organizations" are now being re-marketed under labels such as "communities of practice" or "crowds of wisdom."

Yet this penchant for "the latest and the greatest"—as pointed out by Henry Mintzberg, Bruce Ahlstrand, and Joseph Lampel (Mintzberg/Ahlstrand/Lampel 2009, 11ff.)—not only does injustice to the classical works of organizational research which described decades ago many of the developments that are being peddled as novel approaches today. In particular, it creates the problem that readers are often presented with something which is new but banal, instead of something old which is significant.

The invention of ever new organizational concepts must not be allowed to obscure the fact that the problems have by and larg remained the same. I draw on the verbal excitement in management literature only because, as I discuss the supposedly novel organizational principles, it will enable me to elaborate new insights into the functioning of post-bureaucratic organizations in such a way that they can be linked to discussions among practitioners.

Concerning the Tension between Organizational Theory and Organizational Practice

One could make it easy for oneself and assume that the scientific insights that have been gained into the contradictions, dilemmas, and paradoxes would somehow seep into managerial thinking. This is the hope concealed behind Kurt Lewin's saying, which scientifically oriented consultants enjoy quoting, namely, that there is nothing more practical than a good theory.

At first glance, this seems plausible. Publications by managers and consultants often adorn themselves with the insignia of science. The studies that consulting firms design for marketing purposes are upgraded through a methodology that comes across as scientific. Consultants and managers embellish their articles in professional journals for practitioners with references to scientific literature. And in the meantime, it has simply become part of the job for politicians and corporate executives in some countries to acquire doctoral degrees so they can additionally shine with an emblem of scientific competence. It is only after the doctorates have been revoked on grounds of plagiarism that the executives or politicians explain that the respective ex-PhD was hired as a minister of state or CEO, and not as a scientific research fellow.

In spite of the linkage between scientific theory and extra-scientific practice which is maintained within the display side of organizations, one must not fail to recognize that science, consulting, and management function according to entirely different rationales, and that as a result communication barriers almost inevitably arise. Scientists are oriented toward the production of "pure knowledge"; they do not need to give thought to the way the knowledge is applied. While it is true that consultants profit when they can flag their concepts as scientific, their ultimate concern is whether their concepts match the problems of their clients. For managers, it is basically irrelevant whether the approaches taken also appear convincing in the eyes of organizational scientists. The main thing is that they achieve the desired results in practical terms.

This book is unusual in that it makes a conscious attempt to build a bridge between organizational science and organizational practice without intending to fundamentally remove the tension between the two areas. I am thereby placing expectations on organizational sciences as well as organizational practitioners. Organizational scientists will be confronted with a somewhat unusual form of presentation. This book is based on articles, all of which were first published in scholarly journals and, with their detailed theoretical discussions, methodological explications, and case studies were geared to scientific publication standards. Yet in order to improve the book's readability, the scientific aspects were significantly reduced. I seriously shortened the bibliography, omitted impressive statistics, and dispensed with detailed reproductions of oral citations. In scientific circles, these factors alone represent an obstacle to reception. Yet I can guarantee that if organizational scientists will engage with the uncustomary form of presentation they will find one or another interesting consideration. The expectations I place on organizational practitioners is that they will be confronted with a somewhat unusual view of organizations. My emphasis on paradoxes, dilemmas, and undesired side effects does not fit into the organizational picture normally drawn for practitioners. It is my hope, however, that the descriptions presented here will ultimately align more closely with practitioners' perception of reality than the usual management books that have been trimmed to be streamlined and catchy.

Despite its emphasis on undesired side effects and contradictions, this book also demonstrates why the dream of an optimal organizational structure will persist and that it even has a function. It is only because the boulder always rolls down the mountain just before Sisyphus reaches the peak that he continues to exert his efforts. In his myth about Sisyphus, Albert Camus noted that even though human beings may have been deserted by God, and helplessly and hopelessly thrown back on their own resources, they are happy in spite of the contradictions of human existence. The same applies to executives. They cannot use the undesired side effects, paradoxes, and contradiction along the road to optimal organizational structure as a reason to abandon the search. Rather, it is only by continuing the futile search for optimal organizational structure that the meaning of all the discrepancy emerges.

1.
Introduction: Dealing with the Paradoxes and Dilemmas of New Organizational Forms

"Organizing is when one person writes down the work that other people are doing."
Kurt Tucholsky

The discussion of new organizational structures for businesses, public administrations, universities, hospitals, churches, colleges, and associations or clubs can only be understood against the background of the bureaucratic organization with rigid hierarchical structure, a view that was substantially influenced by the work of Max Weber, Frederick Taylor und Henri Fayol. Even though Weber's considerations about the ideal type of bureaucracy were not intended as a description of the best way for an organization to structure itself, as was the case with Taylor and Fayol, but rather as an analytical method to verify empirical phenomena, all three cases resulted in very convincing descriptions of organizations. Weber's methodologically conceived ideal type and the normative ideal models of Taylor and Fayol are similar in their unmistakable respect for the incisiveness and logical consistency of organizations.

In the work of Weber, and that of Taylor and Fayol as well, one discerns the idea that organizations consist of a rational arrangement of ends and means. According to Max Weber (Weber 1976, 13), instrumental-rational action entails weighing different ends against one another, selecting the most appropriate means for achieving the defined end, and taking into account the possible undesirable side effects that the process of selecting ends and means may entail. In order to reach an instrumental-rational decision in Weber's sense, it is necessary for decision makers to gain clarity about their interests, wishes, and values, gather the most exhaustive information possible about all of the alternative actions, and carefully weigh the consequences of the various choices.

Instrumental rationality does not refer to the fact that players' actions are goal-oriented, but denotes instead that the organization is run from A to Z according to an overarching goal. Using the concept of instrumental rationality, it is possible to construct an entire organization in the form of end-means chains. The leadership of the organization defines a general goal that is to be accomplished. For example, "We want to be number one worldwide in the CD music business." Next, the means are identified through which this top-level goal can be best achieved. For example, "We want to sign a contract with Madonna." The means that have been determined for achieving the top-level goal are, in turn, defined as subgoals, and means are identified to achieve the subgoals. For example, "First, we will sign a contract with Madonna's husband. That will allow us to approach her as well." In this manner, a hierarchical chain develops consisting of superior and subordinate goals with which all activity in the organization can be structured (March/Simon 1958, 191).

1.1 The Linkage between Instrumental-Rational Decision Making and the Bureaucratic Model

It is striking that in Weber's understanding of organizations, but also in Taylor's concept of scientific management and Fayol's administrative management theory, there is a close linkage between instrumental-rational decision making and a bureaucratic or Taylorist ideal type. They held the conviction that there was no form of organization that could compete in terms of rationality (and ultimately performance) with a hierarchically structured and bureaucratically organized enterprise or administration. Much like Taylor and Fayol, Weber (Weber 1976, 128ff.) assumed that the top of the hierarchy identified with the goals of the organization and divided them into many small tasks. A deep, multi-tiered hierarchy organizes the division into precisely defined tasks. The tasks are assigned to people who are most likely to be qualified to fulfill them. Since providing instructions to the lower levels in every individual case would overwhelm the top level of the hierarchy, it establishes programs that inform recipients of the instructions on how they are to behave under normal circumstances. Formalized operating procedures then anchor the programs in organizational memory. Work processes that have been performed are then documented in written files (or later on computers). The leadership level of the hierarchy can concentrate on monitoring compliance and the management of special cases.

Organizational science has repeatedly noted that the bureaucratic ideal type bears a strong resemblance to the functioning of a machine. Much like a machine, a bureaucracy consists of precisely defined individual components acting in clearly determined relationships with the others. All of the individual parts relate to the purpose of the machine and only become meaningful through their integration with the other elements. A v-belt is useless unless it is attached to the rest of the machine, just as a personnel department is only meaningful if it is connected with other departments, say, in a municipal administration. A bureaucracy may consist of a great many individual parts, like a machine, but ultimately its complexity is manageable through precise descriptions of processes. The operating manual for the machine— or the organization's handbook—simply becomes that much thicker. Through external interventions, individual components and their relationships can be changed, thereby adjusting the bureaucracy or machine to meet new requirements.

1.2 A New Idea about the Way an Organizational Structure Looks

In the 1920s and 30s, a critical examination of the bureaucratic Taylorist type of organization began. As a result, a decentralized type gradually appeared on the horizon of possibilities as an optimal organizational structure (Udy 1959).

It seemed to promise greater success if organizations abandoned centralized areas of responsibility and shifted decision making to the lowest possible levels. In strategic questions, decision-making competencies were transferred from the top level to profit centers, sectors, or divisions, which functioned as "organizations within the organization" through a high degree of integration of all functions. In terms of operative orientation, rationalization measures were no longer undertaken only by a specialized staff. Instead, the object was to increase and utilize employee expertise through measures such as continuous improvement processes and quality circles. The hierarchy was flattened by eliminating individual positions and gathering employees into groups and teams.[1]

No later than the 1990s, a decentralized model formed that enjoyed the broad support of various groups in the organization. Managers and heads of works councils, functionaries of the employee and employer associations, experts from such diverse disciplines as business administration, engineering, and work science, and, not least, the business media declared that a decentralized organizational model based on a flat hierarchy, group work, and project work was superior to the bureaucratic ideal model. Surely, never before had such diverse groups endorsed an organizational type so unanimously.

There was talk of a transition from a traditional to a new regulatory framework. People were convinced that the cost advantages of decentralized structures, the growth in professional training of the working population, the development of new technologies, and the demand for emancipation had led to a new regulatory structure which managements could now only elude with difficulty. As a result, the notion of "right action" in management was so compressed in a new regulatory framework that in businesses, public administrations, hospitals, or schools it was self-evident to assume that innovations such as employee empowerment, group work, outsourcing, management by objectives, continuous improvement processes, or profit center structuring were beneficial to the enterprise.

---

1   For early versions, see (Womack/Jones/Ross 1990) or (Hammer/Champy 1993), for later versions of the same, see (Laloux 2014) or (Robertson 2015).

Nevertheless, the notions of a new optimal organizational structure did not lead to an abandonment of the narrow, instrumental-rational understanding of organizations. Even the promoters of decentralized structures generally adhered to an instrumental-rational perspective, except that they simply varied what was viewed as instrumental-rational according to environmental conditions. In a turbulent environment, it was simply more rational to be acting with a decentralized, flat, adhocratic, agile form of organization, whereas in a stable environment, it could very well make sense to revert to something more similar to the bureaucratic ideal type discussed by Weber, Taylor, or Fayol.

We must not overlook the merit of the instrumental-rational interpretation of organizational processes. Research in industrial sociology, work science, organizational psychology, and business administration has had the effect that rationalization processes are being subjected to precise observation, and in scientific circles an intensive debate is underway about how to evaluate the rationalization strategies that have been observed.

The problem with this instrumental-rational approach, however, is that discussion of new forms of organizations has been constrained. In the final analysis, debate on the subject in large sectors of business administration, industrial sociology, economics, and organizational psychology can be pressed into a four-field model. In one respect, the debate revolves around the question of which strategy—one with a centralized or a decentralized orientation—is most likely to contribute to the achievement of an organization's goal. Yet in another respect it is a question of how the centralized or decentralized strategies depicted as rational for the organization present themselves in the eyes of the employees. Do bureaucratic or post-bureaucratic strategies contribute to employee satisfaction, fulfillment, and liberation from alienation, or not? How close is the connection between employee satisfaction and the economic success of their employers?

Within this four-field model there are many opportunities to differentiate. There is debate over whether quality circles belong more to the bureaucratic-Taylorist or the post-bureaucratic model. An argument has arisen over whether discrepancy between the much ballyhooed changes in organizational structure and the actual organizational process results in a pronounced disillusionment effect. One can describe the paradoxical demands that result from decentralized structures and point to the problematical aspects of these new forms of work. One can debate on how the "best way" to reorganize looks in Europe or the US—beyond the scope of Asian rationalization strategies. One can discuss whether extensive partial autonomy or a more restrictive form of group work has a greater effect on increasing employee satisfaction.

Much like the instrumental-rational approach to organizations in general, this debate could be tied into concrete organizational struggles in which managers, employees, employee representatives, and consultants grapple over the way the organization is supposed to look in concrete terms. Since this debate is often conducted with reference to a goal that is viewed as defined (profit, efficient administration, good working conditions, environmental protection), it is easy to link the instrumental-rationally formulated considerations stemming from scientific research to the problems, thoughts, and ideas of practitioners.

1.3 Paradoxes and Dilemmas: A New Focus

The challenge for managers and consultants, but also for researchers, lies in explaining the multitude of paradoxical effects and dilemmas that arise during reorganization processes. Particularly in the late 20th century, the decentralized, dehierarchicalized structure became so dominant (at least in the display side of organizations) that even in scientific research doubting and critical voices were heard only in isolated cases. Currently, however, a deeper understanding of the paradoxes and dilemmas of decentralized, dehierarchicalized organizations is increasing, developing not only in organizations themselves, but especially in the fields of consulting and research.

The concepts of a paradox and a dilemma respectively mark off different problem areas. The concept of a *paradox* indicates a situation in which a statement contains contradictory elements and yet the statement itself claims to be correct. Paradoxical formulations such as "try to be spontaneous" direct one's attention to a special type of truth that has its roots in the obvious contradiction between the two elements of the statement.

The concept of a *dilemma* also points to the difficulties entailed by two opposing alternatives, when there are equally good reasons in favor of both. In contrast to a paradox, which in principle cannot be resolved, the concept of a dilemma places greater emphasis on the pressure an organization experiences to decide in favor of one of the alternatives, even though a recommendation to choose the diametrical opposite appears similarly attractive. Based on demands for consistency and the pressure to act, the contradiction in the perception of decision makers cannot simply be retained, but must be resolved in one direction or the other. The opinion is that a decision favoring one side of the dilemma has to be reached.

It would be an error to conclude that paradoxes and dilemmas arise only in decentralized forms of organizations. Many paradoxical situations have been described in bureaucratic-Taylorist organizations as well. Nevertheless, in "classical" forms of organizations, paradoxes and dilemmas appear to be somewhat controllable through various strategies anchored in factual, time, and social dimensions.

An initial strategy that targeted the *factual dimension* consisted of allowing the formation of local rationalities by creating clearly separated departments and mitigating the resulting conflicts by allocating financial reserves as additional resources. Early on, Richard M. Cyert and James G. March (Cyert/March 1963) pointed out that in hierarchical organizations where the structure is heavily based on the division of labor, goal conflicts can be reduced by assigning the respective competing goals to different units of the organization. The conflicts that exist in the organization itself are transformed into conflicts between departments where they can be reduced by providing sufficient "organizational slack." In this manner, financial reserves can contribute to competing departments not having to arrive at mutual decisions. Intermediate storage facilities reduce quarreling between the production and sales departments because every disturbance does not immediately have an impact on the upstream or downstream department. Since large, bureaucratically structured organizations are especially good at assigning goal conflicts to different units and have the resources to tone down goal conflicts between various units, William H. Starbuck (Starbuck 1988, 67f.) considers these bureaucratic organizations particularly paradox tolerant.

To avoid organizational dilemmas, a second strategy targets the *time dimension* and consists of emphasizing only one side of the dilemma respectively, but also keeping the option open to place the other side at the center the action at a different time. From this perspective, the history of many businesses in the 20th century appears as a permanent, wave-like back and forth movement between two opposing poles. A phase of diversification is followed by a concentration on core competencies. After this, the focus returns to diversification, and subsequently to only a small number of core competencies once again. This dilemma avoidance strategy is based on the assumption that demands from the environment are so predictable and calculable that an organization can concentrate on one side of the dilemma in a given situation (Brunsson/Olsen 1993, 35ff.).

A third strategy aims at the *social dimension*. It consists of reformulating paradoxes, dilemmas, and contradictory demands as problems of the members of the organization. Particularly through the formation of manager roles, fundamental organizational contradictions are translated into personal dilemmas. Branch managers have to reconcile the contradictory demands of higher level management for short-term profitability in their areas of the business on the one hand, and for long-term investment that actually reduces short-term profitability on the other. The master craftsman in the production department has to reconcile the need to maintain an uninterrupted manufacturing process in the face of rapid market changes, and the innovation wishes of strategic management. To a certain degree, the existence of management can be ensured by its adopting paradoxes, dilemmas, and organizational contradictions as its own problem. If conditions in an organization's environment were unambiguous, the CEO could be replaced through a mainframe and middle management through PCs that were linked to it (Luhmann 1964, 214).

Particularly because paradoxes and dilemmas are embedded in organizations, it can sometimes occur in classically structured organizations
that these phenomena escalate in more or less channeled form. Argu-
ments and conflicts between departments, heated debate over a shift
in strategy, or a manager's eruption, "I can't take this circus anymore"
have the effect that paradoxes and contradictions become obvious in
just a few moments.

What we notice, however, is that as decentralization and dehierarchization is discussed, paradoxes and dilemmas also acquire central
significance in organizations' self-descriptions. Increasingly, the task of
management in business enterprises, but also in public administrations,
hospitals, churches, and universities is seen as heightening the organization's perception of complexity by contributing to the development of
dilemmas, paradoxes, and contradictions. The thinking runs that it is
no longer a question, in the sense of James D. Thompson (Thompson
1967, 10ff.), of understanding management as a unit that absorbs
uncertainty and enables a value-adding, technical core to function
according to unequivocal principles, but rather of viewing management
as an entity that develops paradoxes.

For this reason, it is only logical that in recent years managers and
consultants have distanced themselves from viewing paradoxes and
dilemmas as organizational pathologies. In management literature,
approaches are increasingly prevalent which concede that paradoxes
and dilemmas are justified.[2]

---

2   See early (Quinn/Cameron 1988), (Quinn 1988), (Smith/Berg 1997) or (Farson 1997).

2.
The Treachery of One's Own Organizational History

"Perfection of planned layout is achieved only by
institutions on the point of collapse."
Cyril Northcote Parkinson

The introduction of decentralization and dehierarchization poses a paradox. The decentralization and dehierarchization that is supposed to give employees greater influence is not accepted by the respective employees; they receive management's announcements with great mistrust. At first glance, this is an interesting situation. Management grants employees previously unprecedented options. Instead of instructions, there are now mutually agreed-upon targets. Employees can arrange their own working hours and reach decisions independently as to the way they perform their tasks. Methods and procedures can be changed without consulting management. So, from an executive's perspective, it then appears paradoxical that many of the measures which are intended to give employees additional competencies, influence, and power to make decisions encounter such reluctance and in part even resistance in the workforce. The concept of decentralization, which in the meantime is readily touted by organizational leaders and consultants—at least in its systematic form—and is intended to empower employees and provide them with greater decision-making authority, appears to be subverted in many organizations by those very workers.

What causes that? Why is it that many employees are so reluctant to embrace the authority they are offered to organize their work and make their own decisions?

Such resistance is typically explained through technical errors made during the transition process. Examples of reasons cited for the failure of change processes include "a lack of consistency in implementing results," "insufficient information and communication," "deficient analytical and methodical procedure," "inconsistent, halfhearted methods," "incorrect time allowances and target setting," "inadequate professionalism among the participants," "a lack of modeling by top management," too little inclusion of "the people involved," a lack of "courage and endurance," and "rigid adherence to procedure."

These personalizing explanations fall short, however. This chapter will show that the reasons for the objections and resistance in the workforce lie deeper. Using the example of a company in the metalworking industry with a structure generally found in a midsized enterprise, call it Tristan, Inc., we will show why a great deal of friction arose despite the existence of conditions which, in the estimation of executives and consultants, were virtually ideal.

The company was under huge pressure to change because of a decline in orders from its traditional domestic markets, increasing internationalization, falling prices for its standard goods, and aggressive marketing by competitors. The goal of the executive team in charge was to conduct a decentralization process in accordance with cutting-edge change management. It therefore initiated the transition to decentralized structures as part of a design project, supported by consultants and academics.

The change project was conducted under the maxim of very early inclusion of the workforce in the process. It was hoped that this would allow the greatest number of aspects requiring consideration to be integrated, thereby improving the quality of the solutions developed. Furthermore, the idea was to promote insight in to the necessity of change, address conflicts as early as possible, and utilize them for the process. Supporting the project were an internal and also an external consultant who had reached agreement on several basic principles: "never rule against the interests of those involved," because otherwise "conflicts would be preprogrammed"; "the purpose of the method used must be recognizable" because "a lack of transparency leads to resistance"; and, finally, "providing feedback on the results" would be necessary because "otherwise there was a danger of disappointment and frustration."

Even though every effort was made to avoid "technical error," and the process was "perfectly designed" in the eyes of the consultants, the massive resistance observed among employees was striking. The main accusation leveled against management was that its actions were different than originally announced. A number of employees took a defensive stance toward the changes by adopting a "if it's working, leave it alone" attitude, assuming that certain plans would "peter out anyway after a couple of months," or by referring to a previous, similar project that had "gone down the drain." From the perspective of Tristan's head of personnel and organizational development, the workforce had a pronounced culture of "ducking." Employees were simply waiting for the wave of change to wash over them, standing by from a safe position until the process exhausted itself. They were simply holding out until the storm passed.

Based on this company's example, we can elucidate three paradoxes in the transition to decentralized structures which explain employee mistrust of management. Actions or statements are paradoxical when they claim to be correct or logical on the one hand, while containing internal contradictions on the other. Whether consciously or unconsciously, a paradox advances two opposing and contradictory concepts or ideas, yet, unlike a dilemma, it does not allow one to decide in favor of one of two poles.

Using the three paradoxes, we intend to examine the reasons behind the often observed claim of logical consistency in decentralization processes. The object will be to show that the discrepancy between words and deeds in decentralization processes cannot be traced to technical management errors and that socialization in hierarchical structures cannot be held responsible for employee resistance. Instead, the very history of the organization leads to paradoxical situations that can no longer be resolved by increasing communication or participation.

The following part (2.1) discusses the tendency of organizations to introduce decentralized structures in a centralized fashion. When the directive to "Be independent!" comes from above, it strikes employees as paradoxical. In the second part (2.2), we elaborate that although employees do acquire new decision-making authority over the course of decentralization processes, the leadership of the organization continues to have the authority to recentralize decisions that have been reached in a decentralized fashion. The paradox of "decide-for-yourself-but-only-if" arises when a hierarchy (albeit flattened) persists in decentralized organizations. The third part (2.3) analyzes the phenomenon that over the course of decentralization processes employees' self-organization is introduced as something new, which implies that the previously existing informal and often illegal adaptations to regulations are not recognized as a form of self-organization. Finally, the fourth part (2.4) addresses the topic of how managers and employees pass demands for paradoxical behavior back and forth to one another. Yet this game must not be viewed as a case of collective schizophrenia. Rather, it can be viewed as a process of permanent collective self-understanding.

2.1 The "Be Independent" Paradox: The Centralistic Introduction of Decentralized Structures

It is striking that as a rule the initiative to implement decentralized structures comes from business owners, the CEO, or top-level executives. There are hardly any reports in the literature of cases where decentralization measures were set in motion by "ordinary employees."

Centralistic initiation and so-called "process forcing" as a concept of decentralization have often been criticized. Michael Hammer, one of the founders of business process reengineering, declared it paradoxical how autocratically, undemocratically, and from the top down the introduction of the reengineering process often occurs (Hammer cited in Vansina/Taillieu 1996, 32). The pioneering thinkers of the group work discussion, Wolfgang Kötter and Gerd Kullmann, lament that the changes to structures and processes that tend to be based on decentralized self-regulation are decided and initiated in the existing centralistic manner. The definition of the task and the determination of the goal take place in the framework of the old, hierarchical organizational structures that are based on the division of labor, which results in the transition from a hierarchical-centralistic organization, to one that is capable of learning, being planned out in detail well beforehand (Kötter/Kullmann 1996, 42).

In enterprises organized along Taylorist lines, management, not the workforce, was the driving power behind change processes, and this did not create any paradoxes. A manager could "hand down" desired changes, say, the introduction of a new assembly line or the installation of new software, and have the modifications performed "on-site." The innovation that was initiated from above was operationalized by employees in project groups and then, following consultation with the executive, implemented in the form desired.

Nevertheless, a paradox arises the moment it is no longer a question of introducing new software, a new machine, or product, but of implementing decentralized forms of organization. Employees perceive decentralization processes that are initiated and imposed from above as ambiguous. On one hand, they hear the message that employees will now have substantially more influence and authority, while on the other the message is being announced through the customary chain of command, over which employees have no influence.

The contradiction that employees perceive resembles demanding that someone who is tense "be spontaneous," telling a child "I want you to be independent," or encouraging employees in a major corporation to "be entrepreneurial," or "take responsibility." Such instructions are paradoxical because if you comply with the demand to be independent or spontaneous and assume responsibility for yourself, then you are not acting independently or spontaneously or assuming responsibility. Yet on the other hand, one also cannot oppose the demands without experiencing conflict. Remaining in a state of dependence as opposition to the order would be illogical because such resistance would represent a form of autonomy and self-reliant entrepreneurial behavior. Employees who are confronted in this manner find themselves in the situation the ancient Greeks called "aporia," that is, a logical impasse.

The paradox lies in the contradiction between what the communication demands, and the fact that the communication is demanding it. All communication, as portrayed by Niklas Luhmann (Luhmann 2000, 123ff.) in somewhat older communication scientific literature, consists of a *report aspect* and a *command aspect*. On the one hand it communicates content (the report), and on the other it conveys the expectation that the statement is accepted as correct and purposeful (the command). In organizational practice, the report and command aspects cannot be differentiated easily.

Since report and command aspects cannot be separated, popular prescriptions such as "the participation of those affected" or "more communication" seem to be somewhat helpless reactions to the paradox. At Tristan, an attempt was made to avoid a centralistic introduction of decentralized structures by requiring that the employees be included intensively and at an early stage. This requirement conforms with the bulk of the professional literature, where the claim is advanced that early inclusion of employees reduces resistance to change, leads to more practically oriented solutions, boosts motivation, and increases identification with the company.

This argumentation suggests that the centralistic introduction of decentralized structures does not pose a paradox, but is simply the result of not involving employees sufficiently beforehand. Yet this fails to see that requiring participation merely restructures the paradox. Stating that "I am including you in the process I have initiated" is ultimately only a diluted variation on "be independent." The "participation of someone in something" continues to connote a specified measure that has been dictated from above and in which one has been ordered to take part.

My proposal, therefore, is that the centralistic approach to carrying out change processes cannot be traced to failure on the part of management, but is instead a logical consequence of the way the change process has been planned. The "practice" of initiating, planning, and forcing through a change process from above is not "bad practice," but can be understood as the way hierarchically led businesses function. Why is that?

At Tristan, Inc., managers reported that impulses for change always had to come from them. The employees didn't even notice that a sector, department, or the company itself needed to advance in order to survive in the market. This complaint by managers is understandable, but ultimately it does not come as a complete surprise. The "classical" corporation is structured in such a way that production, the technical core of the enterprise, is protected against undue agitation by turbulent changes in the market or problems on the supply side. The task of middle management (which also justifies its existence) is to cushion as adeptly as possible the effect of market turbulence on production and to allow changes to filter into the productive core only in amounts that are easy to process.

Even if many companies attempt to simulate the pressure of the market on the technical core by homing in on certain product groups, process lines, and group work, the technical core by and large remains insulated from the market. The very existence of mid-level managers or sales and purchasing departments as primary contacts with the environment leads to an insulation of the technical core against external pressures. From this perspective, it is not surprising that pressure from the market is registered primarily by management. Consequently, it is also managers who, for the most part, realize that change has become necessary.

Due to their location, employees working in the protected technical core are not able to recognize that a transition to more flexible and innovation-friendly structures could be necessary. Naturally, they allow themselves to become involved in specific instances when they receive instructions from their manager. But in light of their protected status, it is not surprising that they are the retarding element in change processes.

There is some evidence that the "be independent" paradox is exacerbated in organizations that were at one time organized along strict centralistic and hierarchical lines. In these organizations it is to be expected that the paradoxical appeal-like character of management is especially pronounced. Due to middle management's strong specialization on market perception, the sensitivity of the technical core to changes in the environment is particularly low, and the dictation of decentralized structures presumably represents the sole reorganization strategy possible.

Thus, the traditional instruments are the only means available to push through a transition to innovative, flexible, adaptive structures and direct, open flows of information. The flexibility- and innovation-oriented structures that are intended to constitute decentralized self-regulation must therefore be established through the use of the current centralistic approach. An expression of the situation can be seen in the tendency of many organizations to "plan out in detail" their transition from a hierarchical-centralistic organization to a flexible, adaptive structure. Putting it bluntly, under these circumstances the directive to "be independent" must amount to ordering a new flexibility-oriented and self-determined organizational culture from the top down.

2.2 The "Decide-On-Your-Own-But-Only-If" Paradox: Management Lets *Them* Decide

Management literature is propagating a new image of executives. Using buzzwords such as "competence and responsibility," "trust-based collaboration," and "waiving power" it is being proclaimed that empowering employees leads to "independent, self-organized, and productive work." Executives are supposed to "focus on accomplishing new and important tasks" for which they "do not have time under other circumstances." In light of "imponderable and complex factors," managers ultimately have to stand back from managing, that is, refrain from wanting to be in charge. Executives are no longer "movers and shakers" who plan and control everything, but now become facilitators, teammates, or expeditors.

From this vantage point, the ideal modern manager is a person who merely supports self-organization and decision making by an organization's employees. Executives remain in the background, moderate processes, provide advice on difficult questions, and help coordinate self-organization. Ideal change managers then no longer appear as superiors who are cut from classical cloth, but as action facilitators. In the final analysis, they are evaluated only in terms of how successfully they supported transition and according to how well their employees succeed in working more productively and innovatively in self-organized processes.

Until now, management literature has ignored that the systematic implementation of this leadership concept would entail substantial consequences. Executives who successfully introduced self-organization into their areas of responsibility would ultimately render themselves superfluous. Those who truly delivered total quality by enabling the complete self-organization and self-responsibility of their employees, would immediately become redundant. After all, the key to self-organization and self-responsibility is that there is no longer any "meddle-management." Managers who are cut from modern cloth therefore increasingly suffer from the basic dilemma of all physicians, therapists, and development helpers: what ultimately justifies their existence is their own inability to meet certain high demands. If these professions were genuinely 100% successful, they would become superfluous, or at least have to completely redefine themselves.

Nevertheless, particularly managers who are engaged in comprehensive change processes do not complain about having too little work, but rather too much. The specific factor involved in the transition from hierarchical-centralized to self-organized decentralized structures appears to be that executives are responsible not merely for facilitating the process, but for making decisions as experts, too. In the final analysis, managers are hybrids during this transitional phase, granting their employees greater decision-making authority, while also rendering decisions of their own.

At Tristan, Inc., the main accusation leveled at the executives in charge was that their actions were contradictory. Employees complained that while managers were proclaiming their aspiration to empower employees, they were also calling the shots. In questions such as the introduction of a process line organization or the relocation of the custom-made product division, it was unclear whether the decision would be made in the executive suite, or whether it was a joint decision that would be reached by employees and executives together.

During a project steering committee meeting, one of the foremen compared the decisions the employees were facing with two people riding in a canoe. Yes, both of them were paddling, but only the one in the back was actually navigating. If the person sitting in the back were to tell the person in front, "OK, now you start steering, too," the person in front would justifiably feel that he was being "taken for a ride" and would answer, "Look, you're the one who's steering, just tell me when you want me to paddle harder." When the consultant countered that the employees didn't even notice when it was their turn to be in the back and "automatically sat down in the front," the employees objected that time after time management reserved the prerogative to grab the wheel.

The situation the employees were experiencing bears a resemblance to the paradox of the simultaneous inclusion and exclusion of employees during rationalization processes, which was pointed out by Cornelius Castoriadis (Castoriadis 1998). Castoriadis argues that there is a fundamental contradiction in capitalist societies: employees are treated as both objects of bureaucratic manipulation and as autonomous subjects. In order to retain control, management has no choice but to prevent employees from influencing the production process. At the same time it must also permit staff participation because only the workplace-specific knowledge of employees can ensure that the production process has the necessary flexibility.

At Tristan, the consultants tried to force management into specifying who was to make decisions. Managers were supposed to mark their position on a slide showing a scale of decision-making situations. The scale ranged from "I have not made a decision. You are invited to discuss with me whether something should be done" or "I have decided that we will do something. You are invited to discuss with me what we will do" or "I have decided what we will do. You are invited to discuss the details of the implementation with me" to "I have reached a decision on all aspects, there is nothing to discuss." The slide suggested that the framework of a decision could be defined unambiguously. The hybrid position of the executives was to be resolved by management determining which decisions would continue to be made by executives and which by the employees themselves.

Defining a decision-making situation is more complicated than the slides suggest, however. First, the context of organizational decisions is in constant flux. Organizations themselves assert that when environmental conditions are changing rapidly, it becomes increasingly important to react in a flexible way and if necessary to plot a logical new course. Under these circumstances, the central task of management is to improve. Although management tasks have always required improvisation, conditions of uncertainty, according to the tenor of management literature, give rise to a new understanding of managerial action. Second, the transition to an organization characterized by self-organization and self-responsibility is a dynamic process. Perhaps something that is currently still a matter for the boss is at a later point supposed to become a decision that will be reached by employees and management jointly. In the foreseeable future, questions that today are still decided by employees together with the master craftsmen will be decided by the group itself. The transition to self-organization and self-responsibility is a process in which it is difficult to define the framework of a decision in precise terms. For example, in the process under examination, the problem was that the executive aspired to allowing employees increasingly to make their own decisions, while at the same time also having an interest in establishing the model she favored.

Third, there are certain decisions management can only make by itself because, due to the constellation in the organization, otherwise the decisions could not be reached at all. This is the case when a given step toward greater self-organization and self-responsibility runs counter to the individual, short-term interests of a large number of employees. As an example, for many employees it initially represents a loss of status when specialty departments are dismantled and reassigned to other production areas. To illustrate, consolidating installers and component producers in the same group threatens the specific identity of the component producers as highly skilled craftsmen. If decisions of that kind were made subject to self- organization as a matter of principle, they would presumably not be made at all.

These three aspects point to a central reason for repeated management interventions, namely, they are associated with the integration of the decentralization process in a hierarchy that has indeed been flattened, but continues to exist nevertheless. It is specific to an organizational hierarchy that every subject can be taken up to a higher level if necessary. While it is correct that hierarchies only take the step of appropriating decentralized responsibility under exceptional circumstances, they always retain the formal right and, in principle, the option to escalate any decision situated at a lower level and declare a problem to be "a matter for the boss." Even when decisions are ceded to decentralized units, the leadership of the organization can resort to its enforceable managerial authority and revoke participation in the decision-making process.

This option of being able to "take decisions up to a higher level" in principle entails consequences for the assignment of responsibility in hierarchies. Nils Brunsson (Brunsson 1989, 182) pointed out various strategies that players use to reduce responsibility. For example, decision-makers can act as if their decisions were, so to speak, based on automatic causal relationships that are supported by common goals and values. A further means of rendering one's role invisible as a decision-maker consists of foregoing the formal rituals of reaching a decision. Further, one can reduce one's own responsibility through the size of the group of decision-makers: referring to a majority decision made by a large group enables one to portray one's own responsibility as minor. In critical situations, decision-makers can also feign ignorance, because then no responsibility can be attributed to them.

Interestingly, although such strategies of deflecting responsibility function in horizontal relationships, they are significantly reduced through hierarchical structures. Since every topic can be relegated to a higher level in a hierarchical organization, it is impossible for executives to extricate themselves by referring to the responsibility of the units that are subordinate to them. Such executives would immediately face the question (and the accusation) of why they did not draw on their hierarchical authority to intervene in a crisis situation. Shifting the responsibility for the decision from themselves to their "self-organized employees" would never stand as an acceptable excuse. Claiming ignorance would likewise be unacceptable as long as the decision was made in the area under their purview.

Contrary to the postulates of management literature, there are good reasons to assert that decentralization does *not* reduce the responsibility of hierarchically superior executives. Even in organizations with decentralized structures, managers ultimately continue to be answerable for decisions that are made by self-organized teams, autonomous profit centers, or even geographically distant and legally independent networked companies. This is the basis for the right and also the temptation for executives to intervene in the work of self-organized teams.

From a management perspective, decentralization gives rise to increasingly frequent discrepancy between their assigned responsibilities and their actual options. A manager's employees gradually begin to make certain decisions on their own, but the executive no longer has access to all of the information. As the employees become progressively powerful in certain processes, managers find it ever more difficult to assert their ideas. Yet at the same time, their own superiors continue to act as if the managers themselves were responsible for the (good or bad) decisions their employees have made.

Fritz B. Simon (Simon 1997, 140) observed behaviors in managers that were similar to parents. Just as parents have little control over what their children do, managers seem to have little control over the decisions that are made in a business, profit center, or an autonomous team. There is a tendency for managers as well as parents to find themselves in situations where they are held responsible for something they are in fact unable to control, and then react with severe interventions in the decision-making authority of those who bear the actual responsibility.

Such behavior has to be perceived as highly contradictory by employees (and children). "Are we doing it on our own now, or is the shop foreman still in on the decision?" "Is that an order, or are you still open to discussion?" "Do we have a say in this change process, or are we just being included in a decision that's already been made?" Employees receive the impression that they are permitted to make their own decisions, but always with reservations. Their own decisions seem to be OK only as long as they do not fundamentally contradict the vision of management.

As we observed at Tristan, Inc., this can result in proactive compliance on the part of employees. They attempt to guess their executives' objectives. At Tristan, this was referred to as the "loyalty trap." Since the executive continues to have the ultimate say, it is difficult for employees to make their own decisions with any self-confidence at all. They know that the executive has both the information and the authority to reach a decision independently, and they must therefore always fear that the executive will compare their decisions with the one she herself has reached. One frequently observed employee reaction is to guess which decision an executive would make if she were in their situation. The department manager reports that he often encounters the attitude, "I'll self-organize to do anything you want, just tell me what you want me to do."

One executive at Tristan characterized the situation as "leadership in a dilemma." Executives who make a case for their own position find themselves in a Catch-22. If, in the course of a discussion, a majority forms for an opposing opinion, one can enter the fray and attempt to hold one's ground: "All you want to do is assert your own objective, so now you're trying to have it confirmed through a supposed discussion—but that isn't going to happen." By contrast, if one engages with the ideas and concepts developed in the discussion, one can easily hear the accusation that, "You have no idea what you want—and that's certainly not what 'leadership' implies."

This process can result in each side, managers and employees, making the other insecure. Drawing on phenomena such as bureaucratization (Crozier 1964) and surveillance (Gouldner 1954), early organizational sociologists pointed out the vicious circles that arise in organizations through the so-called double contingency of players. In an interaction, A makes his behavior contingent on B, who, in turn, makes his behavior contingent on A. Mutual insinuations, expectations, and observations play a central role here. The basic idea is that these factors can escalate into vicious circles in various directions.

The introduction of decentralized decision-making structures can fail if management and employees become involved in a vicious circle of making each other insecure. Due to pressure from their own superiors, executives resort to just-in-case management. They utilize what remains of the hierarchy to "shoot from the hip," legitimizing their actions with claims that you can't make allowances for self-organization when the house is on fire. This creates further insecurity among employees about their decision-making options, and they become less self-confident about using what latitude they have. This, in turn, leads to stronger intervention by management, which initiates a vicious circle of mutual insecurity.

2.3 The "Organize-Yourselves-But-Not-Like-That" Paradox: Jeopardizing Existing Self-Organization

The self-organization rhetoric that has been playing a central role since the 1990s, not only in businesses, but also in public administrations, hospitals, and schools is based on a surprising fundamental assumption: self-organization is propagated as something that must first be introduced into an enterprise. It is something from which employees have been unable to profit from until now. The assumption is that employees must be freed from "foreign rule" and general powerlessness and, depending on the organization, be admitted, invited, accompanied, led, or forced into the realm of self-determination and self-responsibility. Until now, the rhetoric runs, employees have been patronized, their potential has remained unutilized, and their ability to design processes on their own has been neglected. Self-organization represents an opportunity to put such potential to greater use.

The rhetoric of self-organization suggests that there are simple and elegant solutions for problems that have proven virtually intractable until now. We can speak of a kind of "conversion experience" which has "cast a spell over management." Coordination processes that previously had to be planned in a centralized manner and long beforehand can now be handled independently with little effort by those affected. The energy that "went up in smoke in the form of resistance to external determination" now appears to "benefit common interests of its own accord in the form of self-organization." This attribution of significance is derived from analogies with the phenomenon of the spontaneous formation of order that has been researched in the natural sciences. Not infrequently, it contributes to the "mystification of self-organization" as an "invisible ordering mechanism."

This position overlooks countless self-organized processes that are already operating in every organization, no matter how classic and hierarchical. Even the early organizational theory of Chester Barnard (Barnard 1938), which in certain areas remains unsurpassed to this day, distanced itself from the normative organizational theories of, say, Frederick Taylor or Henri Fayol, to the extent that it did not focus exclusively on formalized processes, but took an interest in actions that reproduced an organization on a daily basis. The formal organizational structure was of interest only to the extent that it directs the everyday "production and reproduction of action into certain channels," "discourages certain communications while encouraging others," and makes "certain communications subject to accountability, and others not" (Baecker 1999, 330ff.).

From this perspective, official hierarchical decision-making channels and rules are not rigid organizational structures that automatically put deviations in the wrong, but rather rules governing distribution of the burden of proof. An action that conforms to the program contains within itself the assumption of correctness and does not require further proof or documentation. Members of the organization do not need to further legitimize an action by arguing that it makes sense. Rather, it is enough to point out that the action complied with the program. A burden of proof is imposed only when members deviate from the rules. Then, the individuals have to hope that their superiors will consider the action reasonable in an organizational sense, and either silently let them get away with it or even officially approve it.

Such "irregular" self-organization processes that occur outside of formalized structures are characterized by the fact that they are not set down in writing, cannot be measured or openly discussed, and above all cannot be the subject of official approval. Even when a company's external presentation communicates that every production detail has been planned in advance, that decision-making channels are clearly defined, that there is a system in place to track every piece of material, and an official corporate culture has been set down in the form of corporate guidelines, life on the inside looks very different. The machinery in the production area is inconspicuously manipulated; failure to comply with certain compulsory communication channels is a regular feature. An internal pecking order, a type of informal hierarchy, develops among skilled workers who are all equal in a formal sense and should only listen to their foremen. In defiance of a virtually perfect tracking system, components and tools are circulating that do not appear on any list. Employees form their own collective identities based on their assignments, personal relationships, and local origins.

The copious research conducted on informality in organizations is to be credited with pointing out the functionality of deviations from the rules. Pointedly formulating the insights of organizational research on informality, Erhard Friedberg (Friedberg 1993, 147f.) argued that a hierarchy that made a program of rigorously enforcing regulations would paralyze an organization. Rules can only be meaningful for an organization, he believed, if the hierarchy adopts a selective tolerance for infractions. The prerequisite for the effectiveness of formal organization is having the option to break formal rules. According to Friedberg, Taylorist organization can prevail for the sole reason that it is repeatedly circumvented in operational practice. If workers and employees geared the performance of their daily tasks to the official system, the results would be chaotic.

At Tristan, Inc., it was also clear that the old Taylorist structure could only function because employees self-organized to repeatedly deviate from the official rules. For example, the company struggled with the typical problems of program- controlled production. It was always producing exactly the wrong thing; the production process was constantly being rearranged; the warehouses were full but the parts required at any given moment were never on hand. Important tools were not always immediately available because of complicated ordering procedures. The employees reacted to these problems with "illegal" self-organization. In order to maintain the production process in spite of the dysfunctionality, there was an officially forbidden hunt for missing parts, "gray" inventories were maintained to ensure the availability of important components, and hidden tool reserves were created.

As an example, the business had developed a kanban system that was intended to ensure continual availability of frequently required components with as little friction as possible. Employees in production and assembly had four crates of components. When three of the crates were empty, a signal was automatically sent to the supplier indicating that new components were required. Yet since this did not always function smoothly, the employees squeezed the components from the various crates together into just one so that the three empty crates would trigger a re-supply order as early as possible.

When management announces the introduction of self-organization in a company using slides, videos, and brochures, the firm's current informal self-organization processes are not taken seriously enough. In fact, it can become even more difficult to recognize informal self-organization as such. The fact is ignored that by introducing self-organization, management is not designing a new organization, but that the self-organization management is propagating represents an attempt to disrupt existing forms.

All of this still does not constitute a fundamental paradox or dilemma. Initially, it is primarily a question of language and observation: management could speak of "new forms of self-organization" and would thereby acknowledge, at least verbally, current forms of self-organization for what they are. The fundamental paradox arises because many of the measures management requires pose threats to long-standing forms of self-organization and, in principle, even challenge their very existence. Measures such as the decentralization of decision-making authority and the creation of self-governing teams generally target the structural problems of a business that is hierarchically organized and based on the division of labor—in other words, precisely those areas where illegal forms of self-organization have previously arisen.

At Tristan, this emerged clearly in several areas. The new organizational orientation toward processes and products, which was intended to make certain forms of self-organization possible, posed a challenge to the internal pecking order, that is, the informal working relationships that had been created through self-organization. The incorporation of task allocators into various process lines abolished forms of internal cooperation which had been laboriously developed through the employees' own initiative. The introduction of an expanded and improved kanban system was intended to provide greater freedom of access to materials. Yet this posed a challenge to the system employees had already developed for themselves: the use of "gray" components for which there was no record whatsoever. The identity encouraged at the top level, namely, viewing oneself as part of a customer-oriented department that performed its work through a significant degree of self-organization, threatened all of the identities which had arisen of their own accord over an extended period of time. It jeopardized the pronounced identity of the component producers in the production department and robbed the "artisans" in custom manufacturing of their special role in the company.

Since the measures that management promotes as new forms of self-organization intrude into processes that have arisen independently, it becomes almost unavoidable that employees perceive the actions of management as contradictory. Suddenly, an executive is telling employees to design the process themselves, but is thereby actually throwing into question the very processes the employees have put in place on their own initiative. In the final analysis, management—which to date has shown no particular interest in employees' organizational abilities—is now encouraging them to organize themselves, but not in the way they have until now, if you please. The message employees receive is therefore tantamount to: organize yourselves, just not like that, OK?

2.4 Paradoxes: Escalation or Resolution

The three fundamental problems discussed above are deliberately meant to contrast with the general trend in management literature where simple explanations and solutions, rather than paradoxes, are worked out. It may be a frustrating experience for managers that the three paradoxes are unavoidable in change processes. A large amount of internal communication, a certain measure of security for employees in the form of time-limited employment guarantees, and a high degree of personal integrity in executives are all factors that can indeed cushion, but never entirely resolve the paradoxes.

In view of these paradoxes, there is a danger that fundamental change processes in organizations are repeatedly aborted without those who are involved becoming aware of the deeper, underlying reasons. This can create an atmosphere in which managements is on the verge of despair over employee resistance, while employees perceive the actions of management as consistently contradictory. Taking the perspective of individual psychology, one can then point out that people have a limited ability to process paradoxes, and the escalation of paradoxes into schizophrenia can be presented as a menacing scenario.

Although describing the consequences of paradoxes may be justified from a psychological perspective, a dramatization is only of limited help in a discussion that focuses on organizations. From an organizationally oriented perspective, the explosiveness of the three paradoxes can be explained by the fact that if it were not for the attempt to transition to decentralized, adaptive, flexible forms of organization, employees would not have the power to block certain fundamental processes in the first place. The big risk could be that employees will reject responsibility for a certain process that management suggests they assume, while at the same time exploiting their new influence to brush off certain technical inputs from an executive. The manager is then in limbo: on the one hand, the employees do not yet feel responsible for the process, while on the other they are using their new power to obstruct the executive's technical suggestions, which previously could have been pushed through hierarchically.

Nevertheless, one can also see a positive side to these problems. There is some evidence suggesting that employees hand back the paradoxes described above to the executives. References to "managerial inconsistency" or the creation of "loyalty traps" can be viewed as evidence that employees are "staying cool" about confronting the paradoxes. An increasing number of situations arise where employees and management mutually confront one another with demands for paradoxical behavior without its having an incapacitating effect on their ability to work.

3.
The Myths Surrounding "Entrepreneurial" Employees

"There was only one catch and that was Catch-22, which specified that a concern for one's own safety in the face of dangers that were real and immediate was the process of a rational mind. Orr was crazy and could be grounded. All he had to do was ask; and as soon as he did, he would no longer be crazy and would have to fly more missions. Orr would be crazy to fly more missions and sane if he didn't, but if he was sane he had to fly them. If he flew them he was crazy and didn't have to; but if he didn't want to he was sane and had to."

An excerpt from Joseph Heller's *Catch-22*, a book about a fighter pilot who was unable to have himself grounded from further sorties, even though he was "crazy."

In neo-liberal economic theory, markets are viewed as a particularly rational form of exchange relationship. Whereas concepts such as hierarchy, bureaucracy, or management have negative connotations of inefficiency and arbitrariness, markets are seen as a particularly effective and just form of distributing goods. The insinuation is that self-regulating markets are particularly good at the division of labor in society, and that central agencies should keep out of market processes to the greatest extent possible.

For a number of years, markets have also increasingly been popularized as a pivotal tool for internally structuring not only businesses, but also public administrations, hospitals, and even universities. Catchwords such as "organizational networks," "marketization," "market-driven decentralization," the "internalization of the market," and "strategic decentralization" are being used to cast competition between organizational units of various sizes as a tool for internal organizational coordination. Management simulates a kind of capital market in the relationship between organizational leadership and decentralized units, and promotes the formation of internal employment-, executive-, resource-, and product-markets.

The principle of marketization was initially applied almost exclusively to the relationship between the central office and the company's subunits such as manufacturing facilities, profit centers, or partially autonomous groups. In the meantime, the concept is increasingly being promoted as a model for the relationship between organizations and their employees as well as employees among themselves. Concepts such as that of the "intrapreneur," a "one-man business," or a "Self, Inc." are being used to indicate that members of an organization are no longer acting as employees—organizational or company people—but as quasi "entrepreneurs within a business."

In management literature, these ideas are used to proclaim that entrepreneurial behavior is expected of every employee. After all, so the logic runs, the purpose of a business is to venture, not to underperform. It has been too long that supervisors, vassals of the crown, and bean counters have occupied themselves with ensuring that employees do no more than what their job descriptions permit.

Given the often euphoric sound of management literature when it speaks of intrapreneurs, independent agents, or a "Self, Inc.," the obvious reaction would be to dismiss the propagation of an "entrepreneur within the business" as a colorful new text bubble in the management field, declare it to be nothing more than a demand for fashionably re-costumed employees, and thereby also explain the lack of research on the idea of the intrapreneur. In contrast to profit centers, which in the meantime have been used in many companies as an internal structuring principle, we have to date seen few examples of companies—there is also a dearth of scientific research—whose appearance has been shaped by intrapreneurs, independent agents, or the concept of a Self, Inc. It is only slowly beginning to emerge how a "conglomerate of internal entrepreneurs" can function and the degree to which it differs from a company with employees.

The limited prevalence of the concept notwithstanding, the model of the intrapreneur has in the meantime influenced a significant number of reorganization projects, and effects can already be observed. For example, the concepts of empowerment and also of target agreements are geared to the intrapreneurship model. In this chapter, I take the concepts of the intrapreneur, the independent agent, or a Self, Inc. at their word, which allows me to elucidate structural problem areas that can form when they are introduced even selectively. Three myths of management literature will serve as a starting point for my argumentation: in the first part "Entrepreneurial behavior can be introduced at all levels of an organization simultaneously"; in the second part "Employees as the new holders of power in businesses" (3.2): and in the third part "the concept of intrapreneurship promotes the integration of employees within the organization" (3.3). In the fourth part, I describe the paradoxical behavioral demands that confront employees in marketized businesses (3.4).

3.1 Myth: Entrepreneurial Behavior Can Be Introduced at All Levels of an Organization Simultaneously

In management literature we encounter the idea that marketization should begin in equal measure on all levels of a company, the profit centers, the groups and teams, and individual employees. The natural scientific analogy used for the establishment of market-like principles on all levels of an organization is based on self-similar and self-organizing fractals. The idea behind fractal-oriented management theory is that the decentralized units should adjust to constantly changing circumstances through self-organization. The assumption is that in these self-organization processes profit centers, groups and teams, and individual employees will become self-similar in the way they function. Every fractal, and therefore in the final analysis, every position, is supposed to function like the entire company. Performance is to be as complete and comprehensive as possible; a task is to be accomplished as independently as possible. Coordination between individual fractals occurs through service relationships that are organized in a market-like manner.

Not Everyone Can Be an Entrepreneur: Contradictions in the Concept of "A Business within a Business"

In management literature, the concepts of the intrapreneur, the independent agent, and a Self, Inc. are constructed as win-win situations. The assumption is that all members of an organization can profit from the introduction of entrepreneurial elements into the company, as long as they willingly adhere to entrepreneurial principles. Yet this overlooks that the different intrapreneur constructions in an organization are generally so intertwined with one another that they mutually curtail each other's freedoms. According to an old insight in the social sciences, one person's freedom is another person's insecurity. Even Erich Gutenberg (Gutenberg 1983, 273ff.), one of the founders of business economics in Germany, noted that gaining freedom to act—which ultimately amounts to entrepreneurialism—can only be purchased by waiving such freedom in other areas of an organization.

It becomes especially clear that the intrapreneur concept cannot be implemented smoothly for all of a firm's employees when the situation involves players at different levels of the organization. The freedom to act on one level, does not by any means produce corresponding autonomy at a different level. On the contrary, self-regulation on one level can spell external control on the other. Below, I will elucidate this idea by drawing on the interrelationships between three levels of decentralized companies, namely, profit centers, teams, and individual employees.

First, the *reciprocity between profit centers and employees*. Being appointed the leader of a profit center entails an increase in power, as compared to a classical middle management position. Whereas a department head in production must still come to agreements with his colleagues in quality assurance, purchasing, or construction, the head of a profit center generally controls of all the important functions. It is only because profit center leaders have assumed responsibility for quality, inventory, scheduling, employees, costs, and throughput time, and partially for purchasing and sales as well, that they can be held responsible for the resulting profits or losses.

Nevertheless, the creation of such minor entrepreneurs at the management level of profit centers does not have to result in their employees becoming intrapreneurs as well. In some cases, the very opposite occurs. Profit centers can develop patriarchal leadership structures, particularly through recourse to the concept of the intrapreneur. Profit centers can develop into little fiefdoms with very strong leaders. Pressure from the company's central office on profit center leaders can have the effect that they feel compelled to intervene directly in the work of their employees and trim their autonomy.

The second point entails the *reciprocity between profit center leaders and their teams*. In the literature, a distinction is made between strategic, market-oriented decentralization and operative decentralization, which addresses concrete work processes. The interrelationship between operative and strategic decentralization is less straightforward than is often suggested.

The leadership of a profit center is given to a manager who is supposed to act like an entrepreneur within the business. This also extends to the ability to make decisions about the profit center's internal structure. If the holding company issues instructions that partially autonomous group work is to be introduced for all profit center employees as a means of encouraging them to think entrepreneurially, leaders of profit centers can perceive this as a limitation of their own autonomy. They might point out that they can only act entrepreneurially if they themselves determine how their profit centers are organized. It can then happen that general managers deploy or disband teams almost arbitrarily and justify such actions by citing their own entrepreneurial autonomy.

In conclusion, we will take a look at the third *interrelationship, namely, between teams and employees*. For many years, it was assumed in the literature that working in groups and teams also increased the scope of action for individual employees. Group work, in particular, was viewed as a logical extension of job enlargement concepts. Yet even in the early 1980s, the criticism was raised that working in partially autonomous groups did not actually amount to freedom from control for their members. It was argued that the autonomy of a group of individuals could not be equated with the autonomy of each individual because the members of the group could suppress one another as well.

In the meantime, a number of empirical studies have shown that pressure on individual employees in partially autonomous groups tends to increase rather than decrease in comparison to classical Taylorist organization. Teams often develop a dynamic that does not exactly result in self-development and social recognition for individual members. Instead, group work is often perceived as a source of aggression, disregard, and bullying. The pressure on members of the group is perceived as even stronger because deviations from group norms can be subject to severe sanctions. Whereas managers in general must adhere to the company's formal catalog of sanctions (warning letters, salary retention, termination) groups can impose informal albeit far more comprehensive sanctions when members step out of line. Since the distribution of power in groups is very diffuse, the sanctioned member has only limited options for complaining to a superior. As well, carrying group conflicts to external sources is often viewed as an un-collegial deviation from the unwritten laws of the group and also entails the threat of sanctions.

Internal Conflicts and Informal Mitigation Processes

What happens when a company tries to use the concept of an "independent operator within the business" to generate autonomy in individual employees at all levels? In my observation, this causes new lines of conflict to form, for which the organization must first laboriously develop mitigation mechanisms.

During the second half of the 20th century, the situation seemed clear: as soon as you had been hired and assumed your duties, you belonged to the company family. You were an "IBM person," an "Amtrak person," a "GM person." All internal career struggles and conflicts during day-to-day work activities notwithstanding, employees could work with stable concepts of friend or foe. Other companies that operated in the same market were seen as competitors. Internal competition was suppressed and a common company identity upheld: "It's us against the rest of the world."

In companies that use concepts such as intrapreneurism in an attempt to steer internal processes through market and competitive mechanisms, the unequivocal friend/foe stereotypes become blurred. Even the early studies of decentralized organizations generally note that a social Darwinist climate arises in such organizations. As a rule, the social Darwinist character expresses itself through conflicts that occur at the same organizational level. Business units and profit centers compete for scarce resources. Various manufacturing facilities owned by the same company find themselves in competition with one another. In part, the internal competition is stronger than competition with external rivals. On the employee level, "I'll-buy-the-world" types face off and conditions among employees become tougher.

Nevertheless, in decentralized organizations the outcome is generally not open, dog-eat-dog warfare. This has less to do with management efforts to (re-)integrate employees (keyword: corporate identity) than with the emergence of informal conflict resolution mechanisms. For example, one can observe that the concept of the intrapreneur undermines notions of partially autonomous group work that have been popular in management circles in recent years. More unconsciously than consciously, an orientation toward "entrepreneurialization of the workplace" amounts to a decision against collaboration in fixed-membership groups. Rather than set teams with clear objectives and permanent members, it appears that the propagation of this concept produces teams that are in permanent flux.

Establishing entrepreneurial behavior on all levels of an organization appears to be an illusion. Even when the entrepreneur is propagated as the central structural feature, informal processes arise that reduce the threat of competition among members of the organization. The demand for entrepreneurial behavior on all levels can therefore be maintained as part of managerial discussions, but in everyday organizational activities it is replaced by more realistic, conflict-diffusing forms of organizing work.

3.2 Myth: Employees as the New Holders of Power in Businesses

For market theoreticians, it may seem paradoxical at first glance that managers call for internal markets, because in the final analysis this would lead to the elimination of their profession. If one subscribes to the logic of liberal market theory, then a market no longer requires a central authority to control it. Hierarchies would erode. The many minor "entrepreneurs within the enterprise" would become the new power holders in businesses and force the bureaucratically oriented managers out of their jobs.

Nevertheless, the managerial profession does not appear to be committing cheerful, unhesitating public suicide. For all their enthusiasm over internal markets, managers are obviously not disappearing from the business landscape. Instead, what the strengthening of market principles appears to be causing is a complex shift in the distribution of power among the players.

The Fiction of Pure Markets

Neoclassical market theories are based on the assumption that markets are places where various providers offer goods and services for sale, and interested, financially sound individuals compare the quality and price of the goods and services presented. According to this view, the coordination of markets takes place solely on the basis of price, which represents all relevant information pertaining to quality, delivery date, and delivery capacity. The outcome is a contract between vendor and buyer which completely specifies performance and consideration.

Such ideal markets appear to be just because the market transactions do not entail entering long-term cooperative relationships. During the transaction, the vendor is interested only in the buyers' solvency (or insolvency), and not in their political views, gender, nationality, or religious affiliation. From this perspective, markets appear to be quasi-democratic models that are based on the motto of "one dollar equals one vote" and dispense with considerations of status and class, religion and morality, and family and friendships. Reflections on dynamizing organizations through internal marketization and competitive principles tie in with this way of thinking. It is argued that in companies that have been reconfigured along these lines, the ability, commitment, and creativity of employees is no longer hampered by managers who earned their positions through accomplishments in the distant past and are now simply exploiting their old boy networks to mutually advance their careers. Instead, it is claimed that an environment has now been created in which every individual, irrespective of gender, national origin, or skin color can compete in an internal market based on performance alone.

In practical terms, however, markets have relatively little to do with the ideal described above. Even Émile Durkheim, the *grand seigneur* of sociology, worked out that the "non-contractual parts of a contract," such as trust, are what enables something like a free market to form. From this perspective, markets do not represent natural phenomena that occur when social processes are given free reign, but are always the results of social construction.

Viewing society as a whole, Karl Polanyi (Polanyi 1957) worked out that the realization of market principles is always accompanied by organized measures to regulate them. Seen in this light, markets do not arise by freeing the economy from governmental interference. Instead, it is the state itself as a central authority that makes it possible for markets to exist. Generally accepted regulatory instruments such as the right of ownership, freedom of contract, and legal certainty restrain free market activity, thereby enabling markets to function in the first place.

In the meantime, various empirical studies have shown the form in which market transactions are embedded in a large number of non-market processes. Even for supposed prototypes of markets such as options exchanges or agricultural auction markets, it has been shown that the personal relationships of the traders exert a strong influence on transactions (as examples, see Moullet 1983; Baker 1990). Indeed, on stock exchanges the existence of money as a means of exchange has not made direct negotiation dispensable or led to a de-politicization of the act of exchanging itself. In light of this embedding of markets, researchers speak of the fiction or the myth of pure markets and call for observing markets in their actual, concrete form (as prominent proponents of this view, see White/ Eccles 1986, 135; Friedberg 1993, 128). It therefore seems obvious to ask how the internal markets are structured in which intrapreneurs, independent agents, and the Self, Inc.s are operating.

The Differences between Internal and External Markets

Particularly since markets are socially embedded, it is necessary to elaborate the differences between external and internal markets. The boundaries of a business have the effect that relationships in the internal markets are organized entirely differently than market relationships with suppliers, customers, or partner companies. The theory of the social construction of markets must be understood more as a call for differentiation rather than a blurring of boundaries. Drawing on three characteristics, namely, goals, memberships, and hierarchies, allows us to demonstrate that it makes a fundamental difference whether a market exists in the social subsystem of the economy or within an organization.

First, we will examine the importance of *goals*. In contrast to the societies of the ancient world and the Middle Ages, modern societies refrain from committing themselves to superordinate goals such as the happiness of the population, racial purity, or fulfilling the will of God. Accordingly, markets, as an important tool for coordinating the economic subsystem of society, are also not subordinate to a higher purpose. Complaints about "economic terror" are prime indications that markets develop a life of their own and elude all forms of higher human purpose.

In organizations, the situation is very different. Regardless of whether it involves a government agency, a high-tech company, or a labor union, goals such as a more or less courteous response to applications for identification cards, penetrating a market with a new, superlight cell phone, or signing a labor agreement with steep pay increases play a central role in orienting an organization (Luhmann 1973, 87ff.). This pivotal connection between organizations and purposes explains why internal markets are far more goal driven than external ones. In the case of internal markets, business units, profit centers, or manufacturing facilities cannot assume that staying in the black will guarantee that they will continue to be part of the company and therewith remain on the internal markets. Exceptional performance likewise does not guarantee that a business will keep an intrapreneur or an independent operator. Driven onward by strategy consultants, companies are continuously changing their core competencies and redefining their goals. If internal market participants no longer fit the goal that has currently been negotiated, they are removed from internal market processes, irrespective of their performance. After all, the motto in companies is not, "Do whatever you like, just generate profit," but rather "Do whatever you like, just generate profit—and keep in step with the company's (changing) goals."

Nevertheless, the opposite process can also be observed. A profit center can continue to exist in a company even if it generates losses over a number of years. Whereas such loss-generating "companies" would soon be bankrupt in a free market, under circumstances they may live on in an internal market, for example, when cross-financing from successful profit centers is ordered. The underlying reason for this development is that business owners do not gear their activities exclusively to the goal of profitability. Instead, motives such as personal fulfillment or a Christian mission can also play a role.

In addition to purposes, *memberships* are important factors in organizations; this, too, in contrast to society overall. A complete exclusion from modern society takes place only in exceptional cases. Most modern nations abstain from deprivation of citizenship. Capital punishment, as the most radical form of exclusion, is practiced in very few "civilized" countries (or could we perhaps say, practiced only in "less civilized" countries) (Luhmann 1995, 16). Initially, "free" markets also abstain from blanket exclusions of individuals as vendors or buyers. A machine builder would be hard pressed for an explanation if he did not sell his machinery to the buyer who offered the highest price. Initially, the potential buyer of a telephone system would in principle not exclude any vendor from the market process. In an official sense, all players can participate in external markets, provided they offer appropriate goods or services.

The situation is entirely different in organizations, where managing membership is a central characteristic. Membership draws a distinct line between those who belong to an organization and those who do not, and that has an effect on internal markets. While management literature suggests that marketability is the only factor that determines the fate of "entrepreneurs within an enterprise," decisions about whether specific elements of a company are retained or not, are made internally. A profit center does not go bankrupt but is shut down or sold. Likewise, an intrapreneur does not file for bankruptcy, but is simply terminated in the classical manner.

It is only the difference between internal and external that makes it possible to prevent the market processes from penetrating unfiltered into various business units, and allows organizations to work with simulated markets instead. Internal markets are constructed in such a way that the performance of a profit center or an intrapreneur can indeed be compared with prices in free markets. But as a rule, the members of an organization are given the opportunity to match the lowest price of external vendors. Intercompany billing prices among individual entrepreneurs in the enterprise do not result from the free play of forces; they are determined by the central office.

Finally, *hierarchies* also play a central role in organizations which, in terms of this characteristic as well, also differ notably from society overall (Luhmann 1997, 834). The times when society was organized according to a strict hierarchy are over. We no longer have a king, emperor, or pope who can project his rule via chains of command or directives into the various areas of the population's life. No one today would accept the President as the highest member of a hierarchy—with the exception of the White House staff.

In contrast to modern societies, however, hierarchies are an essential characteristic of organizations. All dehierarchization and decentralization notwithstanding, we cannot imagine organizations of a more complex type without a hierarchy. It is only their hierarchical structure that enables associations, public administrations, and businesses to act as predictable collective players; it enables external commitments made by leadership to be carried out within the organization through hierarchical instructions.

For internal markets, this means that they do not run counter to hierarchical coordination within the business but are instead an integral part of its hierarchical structure. Hierarchical decisions provide significant structure for internal market mechanisms. The recruitment of employees, their assignment to positions, their termination or promotion, and their salaries are all based on organizationally determined criteria that are essentially defined at the top, and not dictated through any kind of anonymous market mechanisms.

Nevertheless, differentiating between internal and external markets based on goals, memberships, and hierarchies does not allow us to conclude that there is a major bureaucratic conspiracy in the executive suite, lurking behind the marketization of internal processes. It is often overlooked that these decisions are not centralized at the top of the organization. Organizational goals can change without the highest echelons making any strategic decisions. An employee can resign membership if an offer from another firm is more attractive. Even hierarchies can erode without active involvement of company leadership. But one thing is already becoming clear: the concept of the intrapreneur, the independent operator, or a Self, Inc. does not turn employees into the new power holders in an organization.

3.3 Myth: The Concept of Intrapreneurship Promotes the Integration of Employees within the Organization

In management literature, it has been lamented that employees were previously never perceived as important "human capital" and suffered an almost complete lack of recognition as individuals. It was only in the 1970s and 80s that business rhetoric assigned employees a central role. People, it was claimed, were a company's most important resource (Deal/Kennedy 1982). Companies of excellence, the opinion runs, view their employees as the real source of quality and productivity increases (Peters/Waterman 1982).

Management concepts such as the intrapreneur, independent operator, or a Self, Inc. were said to be the only way to integrate employees with all their creativity, productivity, and commitment. Additional room to maneuver would allow employees to achieve greater job satisfaction and thereby stronger identification with the company.

Even if organizational consultants such as Terence E. Deal and Allan A. Kennedy, Thomas J. Peters, and Robert H. Waterman, or their many emulators, dramatically announce the idea that "employees are the most important resource" as an innovation, all they are ultimately doing is recycling a venerable concept from the field of political economy. Even in the writings of Karl Marx, we already encounter the root idea that capitalists can ultimately generate profit only by utilizing the productivity of others.

For this reason, the idea of achieving greater integration of employees through the intrapreneurship concept can be surprising at first glance: what one would expect from entrepreneurs would be autonomization, rather than willing integration into an organized context. After all, an entrepreneur is not an "organization man" or a "corporate man" anymore, but is declared an agent who acts on his or her own behalf. How does it stand then with the integration of intrapreneurs?

The Dilemma of the Simultaneous Integration and Exclusion of Employees

In the past, the example of classical bureaucratic organizations was used to elaborate that the management of companies, public administrations, or hospitals faces a dilemma: it must integrate employees into the organization, while at the same time retaining the option of excluding them. Businesses must deal with the contradictory demands of integrating employees in order to utilize their creativity and commitment, while at the same time also ensuring that they continue to be replaceable so that the business does not become reliant on them. Systems theory argues that organizations, in contrast to families, are based on the principle that people are replaceable. Organizations consist of members who are indeed integrated, but only with part of their selves. In modern society, one does not become a member of an organization lock, stock, and barrel. On the one hand, the only partial integration of employees relieves pressure on them: being terminated by one organization does not entail simultaneous exclusion from others such as a sports club or even society itself. On the other hand, it also takes pressure off the organization which does not need to feel responsible for the employee as a person. The unscrupulousness with which employees are sometimes removed from companies is only possible because human resources managers can be sure that being terminated is not generally tantamount to being shut out of society itself.

The manner in which the integration of employees in businesses, public administration, hospitals, universities, or schools can be arranged without the organization and its employees becoming entangled as companions of fate is the result of day-to-day negotiation processes. Organizations are built in such a way that they can replace employees up to the highest-ranking member without causing the organization itself to fail. The behavioral expectations imposed on employees are determined through their position in the hierarchy and through programs. These factors determine who is supposed to talk with whom, in which manner, and about what. This prevents the organization from becoming dependent on particular individuals. Because of these structures, it is always possible to have a number of people who will deliver a specific behavior. Nevertheless, at the same time organizational processes can never be programmed so precisely that an organization could run like a machine. Organizations depend on the willingness and ability of individual employees to make adjustments, if necessary, to organizational structures in keeping with the achievement of its overall goal.

For the problem of the relationship between the inclusion and exclusion of employees, there is no solution that lasts forever. Instead, the relationship is repeatedly renegotiated. In classical terms, what determines the relationship between the inclusion and exclusion of employees? How does the relationship change when a company attempts to turn its employees into entrepreneurs within the enterprise by introducing concepts such as that of the intrapreneur, the independent operator, or a Self, Inc.?

The Paradox Of "Entrepreneurs within the Enterprise"

Classically speaking, the inclusion and exclusion of employees was tied to the employment contract. Although employers like to complain about the obligations, tribulations, and problems that employment contracts bring on, one cannot overlook that organizations achieve a high degree of flexibility only through employment contracts. Whereas a sales contract involving, say, the purchase of a rare stamp or a package of training seminars, precisely spells out performance and consideration, the terms remain very abstract when employers purchase work through an employment contract. As noted early on by John R. Commons (Commons 1924, 284), employees who sign an employment contract are issuing a kind of blank check and declaring a willingness to put their services, abilities, and creativity to work in keeping with the tasks that are assigned. They waive a detailed, specific stipulation of what their performance is to entail.

The deal between employers and employees is structured in such a way that the employees subordinate themselves to the organization's goals and promise to obey hierarchical instructions. In return, they are compensated by the employer through a salary, stock options, and/or the prospect of career advancement. According to Chester Barnard (Barnard 1938, 167ff.), this creates a "zone of indifference" in employees, a framework in which they cannot say no to instructions, demands, and assignments from their superiors.

The advantage for management is obvious. The employees pledge a kind of across-the-board obedience to as yet unspecified orders and instructions. This allows management to adapt to changing demands very quickly and without cumbersome internal negotiation processes. If every member were granted the ongoing right to contribute their ideas on designing the structure of the organization, flexible, complex structures would never come about.[3]

Nevertheless, management pays a price for the advantage of flexibility—this was elaborated particularly in the so-called labor process debate—in the form of a control and integration problem. Since employment contracts do not specify precisely which tasks an employee is to perform, the employee can attempt to avoid performing them to the greatest extent possible. In contrast to a service contract, where the services to be performed are set forth in detail and the contractor has an interest in performing them in the shortest time possible, it is insinuated that employees attempt to stint on performance. Management reacts to the threat that performance will be withheld by monitoring employees. From this perspective, the entire history of businesses in modern industrial society can be viewed as a struggle to control performance.[4]

When organizations experiment with concepts such as intrapreneurship or a Self, Inc., something important has happened in the relationship between inclusion and exclusion, at least in terms of the organization's display side. Yet what manifestly does not happen in the organization is the replacement of employees through an array of independent business owners or a shift from employment contracts to a multitude of contracts for specific services. Work models such as "independent subcontractors," "pseudo self-employed workers," and "franchisees" are on the rise, but organizations do not appear to be

---

3 There is an entire branch of organizational theory based on the idea of tracing the efficiency of organizations to the fact that using employment contracts as a tool allows them to act without engaging in time-consuming communication processes. As a point of departure, see (Coase 1937).

4 For prominent contributions to the labor process debate, see (Braverman 1974), (Burawoy 1979), and (Edwards 1979).

relying on these models exclusively. A development based entirely on independent subcontractors would result in a loss of flexibility and efficiency potentials. Organizations would lose the flexibility advantages they gain through the instrument of the employment contract. The services to be performed would have to be spelled out in every service contract signed, and it would be extremely laborious for businesses to place a monetary value on each operation and compare it to offers made by other providers.

In contrast to "true" entrepreneurs—and this is an important distinction—"entrepreneurs within an enterprise" are not owners of the relevant means of production for the value they create. The union of "having" (the means of production) and "doing" (performing the services) as it exists in the classical model of self-employment, does not exist for the intrapreneurs or independent operators of the new marketization wave. That explains why the formulation "an entrepreneur within an enterprise" always sounds paradoxical.

In the case of employees as "entrepreneurs within an enterprise," the employment contract as an instrument is augmented through elements of a contract for services. A key form that combines the employment contract with elements of a service contract is the target agreement. This model has existed in organizations for more than 100 years, for example, in the contracts of sales representatives during the first half of the 20th century. Today, however, there is a tendency to apply it to all of an organization's employees.

The Internalization of the Inclusion/Exclusion Dilemma

There is every indication that the dilemma of inclusion and exclusion will not be resolved through the new forms of work, but that the conflict between the two poles is simply shifting to a different area. Stating it bluntly and in simplified terms, in firms that were organized along classical-Taylorist lines, the fronts in the conflict between inclusion and exclusion were clear. On one side, there was management. It was attempting to utilize to the greatest degree possible the employee labor power it had purchased at an all-inclusive rate, yet without becoming involved in a relationship that would make it all too dependent. On the other side, there were the employees. Their interests lay in not expending their manpower entirely, while at the same time making themselves as indispensable as possible to the firm and thereby driving up their own market value.

Again, putting it bluntly, the concepts of an intrapreneur, an independent operator, and a Self, Inc. have a tendency to shift this conflict onto the person of the individual employee. To argue with Michel Foucault, it is no longer necessary to establish control through an omnipresent lord. Instead, the market is elevated to the status of a universal lord who misses nothing, impartially rewards success, and unforbearingly punishes misconduct. For employees, this creates the impression that their failures as intrapreneurs are not being punished by their superiors but by the allegedly "objective consequences" of their own actions. When employees are terminated and parts of a corporation are shut down, it is no longer perceived as an arbitrary decision based on a business owner's profit maximization orientation, but rather as a logical consequence of the internal market.

The introduction of entrepreneurial elements into a company confronts the employees themselves with the problem of inclusion or exclusion. The concept of intrapreneurship combines two opposing interests—the employees, who would actually like to go home, and the boss, who would like to keep them working against their will. In the bureaucratic-Taylorist system the two were neatly split between two different people. While intrapreneurs still don't want to work any longer than necessary, in spite of that, they want to return to their desks after all.

Questions that once represented the classical concerns of top management, suddenly become the concerns of the intrapreneur. Do my activities still fall under the core competencies of the business, or must I develop other abilities? Can the company still afford my activities, or do I have to offer more? Does my labor power still have a value in the current market, or am I simply a burden for the firm?

3.4 Paradoxical Behavioral Requirements in Marketized Organizations

It would be an oversimplification to characterize the concept of an intrapreneur, independent operator, or a Self, Inc. as nothing more than the latest gimmick for managing employees. Certainly, these management concepts are not implemented in businesses on a one-to-one basis. They suggest a logical consistency that cannot be found in practice. Yet these concepts radicalize a development that was already hinted at in the decentralization wave of the 1990s: the contradictory environmental demands that organizations confront are now absorbed only to a limited degree by organizational structures, but are instead passed on to individual employees who perceive them as contradictory behavioral demands that they are required to master.

Organizational sociologist James D. Thompson (Thompson 1967) pointed out that for many years a central organizational strategy consisted of insulating the value-adding core from disturbances or contradictory demands from the external world. Special departments existed which absorbed insecurity, such as operations planning, the personnel office, purchasing, and sales. Consequently, workers on the assembly lines of an automotive supplier, warehouse employees in the mail-order department of a wholesale business, or the staff of a processing department in a government agency could be largely insulated from the imponderables of the environment and supplied with information that for the most part remained constant.

Separation between the departments that absorbed insecurity on one hand, and on the other, a value-adding core that was for the most part kept stable, often resulted in monotonous, dull working conditions for the employees on the assembly line, in the mail-order department, or the processing unit. But it also offered an advantage: they could expect their instructions to be formulated in such a way that they could also be carried out. In principle, exertion of power makes sense only if instructions and orders can be followed. Severity and cruelty are by no means ruled out, and obeying instructions or orders can cause serious damage. In an extreme case, it is actually conceivable that an order can only be carried out if the person who receives it loses his life. Yet even then, it still holds true that the order must be fulfillable. Unfulfillable orders jeopardize the legitimacy of the person who issues them, as well as the entire order-based system. Superiors who issue unfulfillable orders are no longer taken seriously by their employees.

The concepts of intrapreneurship, the independent operator, and the Self, Inc. remove employees' protection against unfulfillable behavioral requirements. There is a tendency to suspend the function of secure roles, which Luhmann in particular pointed out. People no longer know what to expect, what they are allowed to do, and what they are not. There is no longer any protection from the whims of those who wield power in the organization, and no longer any relief from the burden of unlimited responsibility.

4.
Quality: The Paradoxical Effects and Undesired Ancillary Consequences of Quality Management

"When solving our problems, we must make sure
that we do not create ones that are even worse."
Indira Gandhi

Reports from the "quality front" read, in part, as if companies, public administrations, and associations had finally found the magic bullet that will win the battle for better products, more effective processes, and greater employee satisfaction. There are reports of workshop concepts that achieve productivity increases of over 40% and processing time reductions of more than 50% in a matter of days. Continuous improvement processes are presented that urge every employee to make a substantial number of suggestions for improvement every year, thereby enabling a company to save millions.[5]

Based on these remarkable successes, the claim is made that the various quality management tools have led to the discovery of a way to access not only the "gold in the minds of employees" but also the "platinum of the Japanese-inspired rationalization experts." Well organized continuous improvement processes (CIPs) can mobilize the employees' experienced-based knowledge which would otherwise not be brought to bear because of hierarchical organization and the pronounced division of labor. Kaizen campaigns open up the possibility that employees, inspired by the experiences of pioneering businesses, willingly scour their own company in search of problems and weak spots. A well-designed employee sugges-

---

5   An early text that captures the euphoria of quality management measures is the study by (Womack/Jones/Ross 1990).

tion system, it is claimed, brings flaws and waste to light that employees have always been aware of but until now had no way of pointing out.

The current boom in employee- and participation-oriented quality management is closely linked to the decentralization wave that has sloshed through businesses and public administrations during recent decades. It involves more than simply transferring quality competencies to partially autonomous units according to the motto "produce quality through decentralization instead of controlling it through centralization." The humanistic prose often encountered in the literature notwithstanding, from my perspective it would be incorrect to view quality management merely as a step that equips "simple" employees with increasingly decentralized quality competencies and responsibilities.

Rather, quality management has to be understood in the specific context of centralization and decentralization. For central functions, quality management offers the opportunity to gain access to decentralized units "in accordance with the rules." The transfer of competencies to teams, groups, and profit centers in decentralized locations raises a difficulty for their superiors: they can no longer influence the value-creation processes in the same way they could in a Taylorist organization. If one adheres to the decentralization ideology, then superiors make decisions only as to the "what"—that is, the result to be achieved. The "how" is primarily left to the competence of the decentralized units.

In this situation, quality management tools give central positions an opportunity to exert influence on the "how." Granted, continuous improvement processes, kaizen workshops, and quality norm certifications do not allow one to prescribe in precise detail the way a value creation process should look, yet they do create a framework for the organizing of the value creation process. The framework for optimization measures in decentralized locations can be constructed with various degrees of restriction. Quality norm certifications do not prescribe how a process is supposed to be organized, but only that it should be executed in accordance with a precisely defined standard, that clear competencies and responsibilities are defined, and that the process is replicable at any time. Quality circles and continuous improvement processes initiate the elaboration of a certain spectrum of topics, but the nature of the solutions is transferred to the competency of the groups. Kaizen campaigns, meanwhile, specify with significantly greater precision the principles according to which the employees themselves are to implement optimizations.

This chapter will focus on a closer examination of the effects of the various quality management tools. The first part (4.1) shows that transforming informal processes into formalized workflows within the context of a quality management program can be counterproductive. For that reason, quality measures that build on informality, such as an employee suggestion policy, kaizen, and CIP are limited in their effectiveness. In the second part (4.2), I show that the use of several quality management tools does not necessarily lead to integrated quality management, but can instead result in competition between the various tools. The third part (4.3) points out the paradoxical effects caused by referencing the Japan myth. In Europe, referring to Japan served as legitimation for quality management strategies for as long as the Japanese economy was booming. When it collapsed, the close alignment with Japanese practices increasingly had a counterproductive effect on the implementation of quality management measures in businesses. This section presents illustrative examples of the way management concepts are first propagated by referring to successful national economies of the day—first the USA, then Germany, followed by Japan, then China and in the future, perhaps, India, Brazil, or some other country—but immediately become less attractive when such economies begin to show signs of weakness. In the fourth part (4.4), I argue that quality management methods tend to be shaped by the requirements of the consulting firms operating in the market, rather than the needs of the organizations requesting their services. This consideration applies not only to quality management methods, but can also be applied to many of the methods consultants promote for developing strategies or restructuring organizations. The fifth part (4.5) sets forth the functionality of "quality façades." It argues that there can be constellations under which none of the players has an interest in eliminating the façade character of quality management. In part six (4.6), I show what the contours of quality management look like beyond the dream of perfect organizational structures.

4.1 Coming to Terms with Implicit Game Rules: Informality as a Reaction to Paradoxical Behavioral Requirements

Most of the reform projects facilitated by consultants begin with an organization's manifest, visible structures. It is unsurprising that change projects would orient themselves on such structures because they are generally known within the organization and can therefore be readily discussed. This understandable tendency to gear change projects to structures that are clearly evident arises even during a project's initial development phase. Top management needs to have an idea of how many resources the project will involve. The line managers affected by the project would like to know what is supposed to change in their organization. The consultants are interested in having a clearly formulated assignment, so they can calculate their own costs and plan how to deploy their staff.

Quality management projects often use a different point of departure, however. Hidden behind the use of tools such as quality circles, kaizen, and CIP lies the hope of being able to overcome the strict separation of manual work and brain work. The tools used in the 1980s and 1990s, first in the automobile industry and subsequently in almost all sectors, aimed at mobilizing the experience-based knowledge of employees and stood in clear competition to classical rationalization through experts. Instead of shifting the responsibility for quality and rationalization merely to a handful of experts, the idea was to utilize all of the resources that could be mobilized in the company for continuous production improvement, irrespective of their status and function.

Eliminating the strict separation between manual and brain work was intended to address one of the fundamental problems of Taylorist organizations, namely, the discrepancy between the plans devised by experts and the reality of the production process, which functions according to its own specific principles. For that reason, quality circles, kaizen, and CIP as approaches were always directed at restoring the feedback of applied experience gained in the production area to the planning department, and ensuring that hands-on knowledge once again cycled into planning.

The Problems Associated with Converting
Informal Knowledge into Standards

In concrete terms, this involves converting the informal utilization of employees' hands-on experience into formalized standards. The hope is that the solutions individual employees have found through decentralization can be anchored in organizational memory in the form of structure, regulations, or a process. In the view of Masaaki Imai (Imai 1986), the moment a solution has proved itself it becomes one of management's central tasks to disseminate the advantages throughout the entire organization by issuing clear instructions that make the improvement binding.

Nevertheless, this is exactly the point where experience shows that quality management initiatives run into problems. In the framework of a quality campaign, why should employees be enthusiastic about revealing their informal behavior on the job, their hidden room to maneuver, and their performance related reserves? Experience-based knowledge, secret leeway, familiarity with the organization's informal processes, and performance reserves that are kept under wraps, are the trump cards employees play in organizational power struggles. Formalization and standardization pose a threat to employees because the practical experience they have gained becomes common property, and they no longer have a trump to play.

The how and why of resistance against quality management initiatives made its presence felt during a kaizen campaign in a French property management company that we will call Sommet. The central office at Sommet launched a wide-scale kaizen initiative to improve the work quality of their craftsmen teams and increase customer satisfaction. The hope was that the kaizen campaign would enable the central office to push through its specified quality, production, billing, and authorization standards. Thus, the external consultants engaged in various areas received what might be called a dual assignment. On the one hand, they were supposed to mobilize local know-how. On the other, their kaizen workshops were supposed to assist in converting the practical knowledge into standards and thereby establishing it.

As the project unfolded, the internal and external consultants repeatedly encountered considerable resistance from team members against measures that clearly made their work easier. For those who were conducting the kaizen initiative, this came as a surprise. They had assumed that the employees—who enjoyed termination protection—would be interested in optimizing work processes. Yet they overlooked that the rationalization reserves which appeared so obviously unutilized fulfilled critical functions in the individual rationales of the employees.

For example, in one workshop the situation arose that a maintenance team fought tooth and nail against cleaning up a small parts depot. This seemed irrational to the kaizen trainers, because a well-ordered storehouse would have made it easier for all employees to find material. It was only in marginal talks that consultants learned that outside firms also had access to this storehouse if they offered their repair services at a more favorable price than Sommet's team of craftsmen. Since the small parts were officially owned by the client, one could not deny outside firms' access. Thus, the strategy of the in-house team was to permit such a degree of chaos in the storehouse that no one but the storehouse "experts" on their own team could locate the required parts. To a great extent, this prevented the outside providers from retrieving parts, whereas an orderly storehouse in accordance with kaizen notions would have facilitated access for the outside firms, thereby increasing customers' tendency to place orders with them.

In a different workshop, optimizing the physical space situation was on the agenda because all of the employees were complaining about long distances, coordination difficulties, and poor working conditions. The consultants began with the optimization of the "officially" available spaces. Over the course of the workshop, however, the employees showed the consultants—under the pledge of secrecy—that in addition to the six officially rented rooms there were additional 20-30 spaces in the catacombs of the huge property that were being used "illegally." Over the past decades, the maintenance team had repeatedly "appropriated" ventilation rooms, storage space under escalators, former vehicle maintenance areas, and forgotten storage rooms. As the years went by, these spaces had been turned into comfortable individual work areas, some of which had been wallpapered and furnished with rugs and microwave ovens, and allowed the employees to do their work without being disturbed by management or the customer. Neither leaders nor team members were interested in dismantling the illegal spaces because they provided storage and work areas throughout the entire complex. The consultants were given to understand that the spaces they had been shown in confidence did not exist as far as the workshop was concerned, but that the teams would actively participate in the optimization of the official spaces.

In the dominant line of quality management, the existence of such informal behaviors, hidden leeway, and performance relevant reserves would be viewed as a point to begin quality improvement measures. One would address precisely such informal aspects of the organization in order to convert them into formalized (and thereby collectively optimizable) working conditions. Yet this would be to overlook that informality fulfills an important function.

The Functionality of Deviations from the Rules

The struggle against informality which is conducted implicitly in kaizen initiatives and continuous improvement processes, is based on an instrumental-rational understanding of organizations. Supposedly, organizations have an unequivocal purpose and that alignment with it is enforced through hierarchies from the top down. Yet if one assumes instead that organizations are characterized by inconsistency of purpose and brittle hierarchies, then their attempts to contain informality become reminiscent of the quests of Don Quixote. For the most part, organizational scientists agree that formal and informal structures represent two important complementary aspects of organizations. Informality cushions contradictory demands on organizations and thereby compensates for the imperfections in their regulations.

The effect was seen in the case of Sommet described above. When teams were confronted with contradictory demands, informal structures evolved allowing them to solve the dilemmas in which they found themselves. They were required to adhere strictly to comprehensive corporate guidelines, and yet they were expected to fulfill customer requests faster, more flexibly, and at a better price than the small businesses the company was competing with as a building management firm.

An example of a further topic was the company guideline that required obtaining three offers before subcontracting jobs in excess of €500. It became clear relatively quickly that the teams interpreted this regulation very liberally. Sometimes, rather than having several contractors compete for the job, a previously determined provider was instructed—parallel to immediately performing the work—to solicit two additional bids from "cooperating competitors." This practice made it possible to adhere to company guidelines with respect to awarding contracts, at least officially, while at the same time providing the end customer with fast service. Naturally, processing this informality in the workshops was out of the question because it was impossible to formalize the practice of bypassing company guidelines, thereby making it generally visible to one's superiors.

A similar process was noted in stock keeping. Instructions from the central office were that stock should be reduced to a minimum. The reason for the instructions was that there should be no stockpiling in the maintenance department because it entailed high inventory carrying costs and tied up capital. Yet these instructions from the central office conflicted with the interests of the end customers. When a problem arose, customers were unwilling to wait for the delivery of replacement parts and insisted that the local teams have important replacements in stock. This led to the existence of official "white inventory" and informal "black inventory." Since the "black inventory" didn't officially exist, it could be discussed in part but not completely in the presence of employees from the central office. As a result, optimization efforts initially focused on the "white inventory," which was insignificant in terms of figures, whereas the hidden "black inventory" was screened out.

Addressing such informal procedures within the framework of decentralized quality circles, continuous improvement processes, and kaizen workshops is possible only to a limited degree. An attempt to reduce informal behavior, concealed leeway, and performance relevant reserves would have resulted in the teams no longer having a cushion that enabled them to fulfill conflicting demands. If the teams had unwaveringly adhered to the regulations, simultaneously having to fulfill both the conflicting demands of their customers and their own management would have caused them to fail.

Classical quality management ideology purports to have a solution for such conflicting requirements, namely, that one must understand the paradoxical demands as a task for higher positions. All problems that are insoluble at a decentralized level, the thinking runs, must be solved by the person in charge in the central office.

Yet this notion is naïve for two reasons. First, the chairman of a corporation with several hundred thousand employees cannot be confronted with all of the paradox demands they face, simply because one team in a certain unit of a business sector requests a change in company guidelines. Second, and more importantly, it is completely impossible to accommodate every demand in a company without creating contradiction because an organization is always geared to very different environments.

4.2 The Paradoxical Effect of Integrated Quality Management

Following the Second World War, the only quality management tool used in most organizations was the employee suggestion system. In the meantime, many organizations are using an entire palette of various tools: quality circles, CIP, CIP2, kaizen, the Japan Diet, the Balanced Scorecard, Genesis, quality management certification under ISO 9000ff.—or the standards of the European Foundation for Quality Management—it has become almost impossible to list them all.

It is not always clear whether a new tool truly represents a methodological innovation, whether it is something that has been said before and simply received a new label, or whether a consulting company is trying to position a re-mix of different tools in the market as a product of its own. In some companies, for example, we have observed that the quality circle concept that was much criticized in the 1980s was revitalized, first under the heading of CIP groups, and subsequently, when that idea seemed to run out of steam, under the name of kaizen. The methodological innovations that CIP as well as kaizen offered in comparison to quality circles were often lost. Surveying quality management methods becomes even more difficult because concepts that pertained to CIP groups and kaizen workshops, and originated in Japan, were promulgated by consulting firms under trademarked concepts such as VIT, CEDAC, or Genesis.

There are two reasons for using several different quality management tools in parallel: one is manifest and unproblematic to communicate, while the other is latent and less easy to bring up in the organization. The manifest reason is that each tool addresses only one segment of the quality problem. Take CIP groups, for example. While they try to access the "gold in the employees' minds," they generally do not utilize external rationalization know-how. Kaizen workshops on the other hand, address problem areas that have been precisely defined with the help of rationalization experts, but they do not utilize all of the ideas that individual employees develop in their work process. This explains why various quality management tools are often used in combination. The second reason is less easily communicated in an organization: quality management tools gradually wear out. The CIP groups lose their enthusiasm, the quality of the input received through employee suggestion programs declines, and, once the consulting contracts run out, the kaizen workshops are continued only on a modest scale. As their success is no longer measured by monitoring product quality alone, but also according to the degree they are able to sustain permanent process improvements by using newly developed tools, quality management departments show a great willingness to repeatedly try out such new approaches.

The boom in the quality management market has led many organizations to adapt an attitude of "the more the better." The assumption is that quality is like profit or love: you can never have enough of it, and for that reason taking a wide range of quality measures makes sense. Yet quality management tools can conflict with one another, and this is overlooked.

The Competition between an Internal Employee Suggestion System, CIP, and Kaizen: The Case of a Midsize Company

A midsize company—call it Veletto—was working with a number of different quality management tools such as kaizen, CIP, an employee suggestion system, the Japan Diet, and ISO certification. In addition, the company participated in various quality competitions. The employee suggestion system was established early in the days of the company's founder but then fell into a deep sleep, only to be revitalized 20 years later by a new CEO. Word was put out that the number of suggestions for improvement was to be increased by 30% every year. The continuous improvement process was introduced after it came to the company's attention that a "factory of the year" had positive experiences with CIP. In principle, the CIP was conducted like a quality circle under the leadership of internal moderators, and was intended to work on day-to-day operating problems in groups of three to six individuals. Two years after the CIP, the company launched a kaizen initiative. In contrast to the very open processes of the employee suggestion system and CIP, the kaizen was clearly underpinned by a production and assembly ideology. Then, on top of the employee suggestion system, CIP, and kaizen, the Japan Diet was introduced. It consisted of 20 "keys" that were supposed to optimize work in various sectors. Parallel to these processes, the company began to think about gaining ISO certification.

The question is, how did the various quality management measures interact with one another? The basic tenor of many discussion partners at Veletto was that quality management "isn't a bad thing," but that unfortunately it was being "taken too far." One department head remarked, "Do we need all this? Do we need all the hoopla?" On the employee side, meanwhile, it became clear that they were suffering from improvement overload. A different department head commented, "Sometimes they overdo the quality management at the expense of the production process …

Maybe we're doing too much of it—spending too much on consultants and not enough on the ongoing development of our machinery."

The cause of these complaints was the growing competition that had formed between the various improvement measures. As an example, in the CIP workshops employees deliberately did not suggest a number of obvious solutions because they hoped to receive bonuses for submitting them as part of the company suggestion program. When they contributed suggestions that were actually suitable for the company suggestion system, their colleagues let them know that it would be better to hold back.

Conflict also arose between kaizen and the CIP. The kaizen consultant demanded that his initiative should be the basis for resetting the company standards, while CIP would merely be used to fine tune them. Kaizen, he said, was like felling a tree; CIP was what you used to turn it into toothpicks. The propagation of kaizen's hegemony over the organization of production was not accepted, particularly by the department heads. Kaizen was perceived as "coming from the outside," whereas CIP was viewed as an internal project and was especially promoted by the department heads. Conflicts between the different production and reorganization concepts, favored respectively by kaizen and CIP, were always especially pronounced when kaizen and CIP workshops arrived at different solutions for the same problem.

Approaches to Integrating Quality Management:
The Escalation of Conflict

In the main thread of the discussion, conflicts that emerge through the application of different quality management tools are not viewed as an understandable result of functional differentiation in organizations. Rather, they are understood as a call for "optimal coordination of goals and methods, i.e., processes." Concepts such as total quality management, integrative or integrated quality management claim to merge the various quality enhancement tools.[6]

---

6   As an example of this type of thinking, see (Bendell 2006).

Management at midsized Veletto also recognized competition between the various improvement initiatives as a problem and promoted the idea of integrated quality management. "Yes, we're trying. There are a couple of holistic systems that network everything." Each new quality measure was therefore expected to integrate the various other ones. For example, it was hoped that kaizen word be able to integrate initiatives from the CIP and the employee suggestion program. The CEO declared, "The kaizen consultant is the first person we have who's a pro in all of these methods. Up until now, it was all piecemeal, but now Smith is suddenly pulling it all together." The Japan Diet was also associated with the hope that it would lead to a unified approach. Dr. Jones, the diet consultant, would "merge everything into one comprehensive concept," the CEO explained.

Contrary to the CEO's assessment, however, the development observed was that the introduction of new measures, which were actually supposed to promote integration, instead triggered additional conflict and contradictions. Holistic concepts such as kaizen and the Japan Diet brought additional players into the game, and that resulted in new constellations of interest. There was a tendency for new lines of conflict to develop, instead of an integrated concept resulting in fewer conflicts. The attempt to use integrated management concepts to counter the effects of functional differentiation and the local rationalities it produces, appears to be a Sisyphean task—exacerbated by the condition that the stone becomes somewhat heavier with every attempt to move it.

4.3 The Recoil Effect, the Japanese Myth in Quality Management

The andon error notification system, the baka-yoke mistake proofing system, gemba, the kaizen quality philosophy, the heijunka tool for production smoothing, the ishikawa diagram, jidoka, an aid for locating problems, the kanban logistics concept, the kaishain personnel management philosophy, the big three Ms of "muda, mura, muri" as the basis for a philosophy of loss, the five organization principles of "seiri, seiton, seiso, seiketsu und shitsuke," warusa kagen—more Japanese concepts have entered into quality management than hardly any other area of organizations.

For many years, adopting Japanese quality tools was seen in Europe and America as a guarantee for success. Consequently, in a particularly large number of companies reorganization projects were promoted by referring to the Japanese origins of their strategies. As a result, however, many quality measures were linked with a "Japan myth" that became counterproductive as the Japanese economy ran into increasing difficulties.

Myth: Effective and Efficient Quality Management Was Responsible for Japan's Economic Success

How do we explain the popularity of Japanese concepts in European and American quality management? The spread of these concepts is closely related to the success of Japanese businesses in the 1980s and early 1990s. In important areas of the economy such as the automotive, shipbuilding, computer, and electronics industries, Japanese businesses penetrated European and American markets with quality products at comparatively favorable prices. In key sectors such as machine construction, Japanese products at times achieved a market share in excess of 50 percent.

Particularly in the 1980s, a prevalent explanation alleged that the strength of Japanese businesses could be traced to their more industrious, less demanding mentality. It was emphasized that virtues such as punctuality, discipline, diligence, commitment, mutual considerateness, modesty, and politeness played a central role in the Japanese workplace. According to this explanatory approach, the Japanese workplace was characterized by a striving for perfection, harmony, and consensus. Much like Japanese society overall, working life in Japan was permeated by group awareness and a sense of community: group interests ranked higher than the interests of an individual. Furthermore, it was said that the loyalty of Japanese employees toward their employers played a key role; businesses rewarded this with a job for life.

In European and American management circles, this cultural explanation strengthened the attitude that "there wasn't a lot you could do." The key to Japan's success lay in a cultural mentality specific to the nation itself and could not simply be copied by a business in a different country. If one attempted to bring Western work organization more closely into line with the Japanese "company clan model," one had to reckon with a discrepancy between the organizational structure and an individualistic cultural environment.

During the 1980s, the cultural position met with increasing opposition by those who argued that the Japanese organization type could function independently of the special characteristics of Japanese mentality and culture. Reference was made to factories operated by Japanese corporations in America and Europe, and it was maintained that the features of the Japanese organizational model such as group work, kanban, just-in-time relationships, and continuous improvement processes could also be implemented successfully in industrialized Western countries.

In light of this controversy, it is understandable that American and European executives readily embraced any explanation that did not attribute the rise of the Japanese to a specific mentality but rather a particular form of work organization. Their belief that the rise of Japanese corporations was based on a management strategy allowed them to conclude that they could copy, adopt, and further develop these recipes for success, and they hoped to achieve similar outcomes by simply adopting the strategies. Much as was the case with the cutback strategies à la lean management, the impressive achievements of Japanese businesses had the effect that in the field of quality management as well, Japanese approaches were quickly viewed as a potential key to success for European and American businesses.

The notion that the use of Japanese quality and production management methods would lead to success increasingly became a virtually unquestioned hypothesis. A tight cause-and-effect chain was postulated between Japanese quality management and the country's economic success. Other explanations for Japan's boom were screened out of the rationality focus during this phase, for example, Japanese savings behavior, membership in corporate networks, low tax rates, the special characteristics of Japanese unions, and the principles of lifelong employment or working overtime in Japanese factories. Instead of explaining the supposed superiority of Japanese businesses along the lines of "long working hours versus short working hours" or "Japanese versus Western organizational culture," the cross-section of the world was undertaken along the axis of effective Japanese production and quality management versus traditional Taylorist production and quality management in Europe (Ortmann 1994, 144).

Japan's economic success was reduced to concrete aspects of Japanese production and quality management. Soon, the concept of the "Japan myth" began circulating in the business press. Now, the special feature of myths is that they are not entirely fictitious. There can be no doubt that the production model at Toyota contributed its share to the success of the Japanese automobile industry. While myths are only partially based on verifiable facts, they are considered to be true overall.

In many organizations, the "Japanese myth" was used as a "transmission belt" for quality measures. Two "kinds of indirect Japanization" could be differentiated. The first kind aimed at adopting individual forms of Japanese management practices and enriching them with one's own strategies. The second strategy consisted of merely exploiting the appearance of Japanese efficiency as legitimation for one's own change strategy (Ackroyd/Burrell/Hughes/Whitaker 1988).

In the major facilities management corporation, for example, quality management workshops were initially promoted under the concept of kaizen as a way of deliberately referencing Japanese success and thereby generating pressure to change. In the workshops, the consultants bandied Japanese terms such as muri or seiri in order to lend authority to their reorganization measures. At Veletto, a midsized business, an entire quality initiative was run under the heading of the Japan Diet to demonstrate clearly that it was geared to the success recipes used in Japanese industries.

There are inarguable advantages to drawing on simplistic, unexamined cause-and-effect chains and using fiction and dogma. They provide orientation, save time, and allow the accumulation of power. Referencing proven Japanese practice established the framework for the quality measures and shortened the time-consuming discussions of how to proceed. Players who availed themselves of the "Japanese myth" initially built leverage because other players were forced to recognize the superiority, transferability, and potential of the cause-and-effect chains that were being assumed.

The Recoil Effect: Problems in the Japanese Economy

The standard criticism of myths is directed at their excessive distance from reality.

A reemergence of doubt, unexpected events in an organization's environment, or the addition of new players causes a myth to become apparent for what it is, and thereby destroy it. The myth loses its ability to create ignorance and thereby increase the organization's ability to act.

In the case of Japanese quality management, however, a different problem emerges in terms of working with myths. By referencing myths, players commit themselves to cause-and-effect chains which they later cannot readily divest. The quality managers, consultants, and trainers who pointed to Japan to legitimize their measures ran into problems when their assumptions were no longer based on a successful model.

The difficulties in the Japanese economy beginning in the second half of the 1990s can probably no more be traced monocausally to the superiority of European, American, or Chinese production and quality management models, than Japanese success could be explained ten years before solely through the Toyota production model. Observers are justified in pointing out that the paralyzing interwovenness of the major Japanese concerns, an ailing banking system, undesirable political developments, and a value shift in Japanese society are important factors for explaining Japan's economic woes.

For the current discussion of quality management, we are not interested in the causes responsible for Japan's economic problems, but rather in the effect of Japan's poor economy on the use of the "Japan myth" in quality management projects in other countries.

The worse the economic situation became in Japan, the more frequently players in Western firms such as Sommet or Veletto, where there were doubts about the Japanese methods propagated in the companies, began to question the "Japanese myth" in their critical remarks. At Sommet a tradesman raised the question of why they were working with a Japanese quality method like kaizen in the first place. "I mean, the Japanese aren't doing so well." During a discussion about kaizen at Veletto, a rhetorical question was asked: "Can't you just say that in plain German." After all, the argument ran, we have a successful tradition of German craftsmanship, too. If you wanted to revive the "German virtues of orderliness and neatness" there wasn't really any reason to draw on a dubious Japanese success model.

Thus, the promoters of quality management were confronted with the "Japanese myth" in the sense of a cautionary example. In one company, growing resistance to a Japanese project name, which additionally referenced a dubious success model, resulted in a renaming of the project while it was still underway: it was no longer called a "kaizen initiative" but now referred to as a "CIP process." To support the process, one no longer invoked the "Japanese myth" to such a degree, but instead pointed to the alleged successes achieved with the program in other areas of the company.

4.4 Adjusting to the Interests of Consulting Firms' Quality Assurance Departments

A paradoxical situation developed when various tools of Japanese origin were operationalized in European and American corporations. Even though there was always talk of quality circles, kaizen, or the Japan Diet as an expression of a comprehensive idea of quality, the main tools the consulting firms used were one-hour sessions or intensive multi-day workshops during which employees were gathered together.

In many circumstances, regular one-hour meetings and multi-day workshops appear to be extremely effective tools for initiating change processes. They make it possible to gather employees selectively for the purpose of solving precisely defined problems. It is nevertheless striking that at first glance the workshop concept in particular actually contradicts the principle of continuous improvement as demanded by the pope of quality, Masaaki Imai, and others, because it is the very characteristic of workshops that they represent exceptional situations.

How did it come about that kaizen, as a principle of permanent improvement, was reduced primarily to conducting workshops?

Quality Circles and Kaizen—as Adapted to the Way Consulting Firms Function

If you read the way companies describe their quality management programs, you have the impression that implementing them in the form of workshops arises from the requirements of the respective company. It seems that quality management concentrates on meetings and workshops because this is the most effective and efficient way to ensure and improve quality in the individual companies, as well as to anchor the concept of quality in the minds of employees. But are these self-descriptions accurate?

Organizational research has established that many products do not reflect the needs and demands of the client; instead, they are an expression of the internal organizational requirements of the company that is producing them (Legge 2002, 80ff.). To a certain degree, that is also functional. Production that is tailored exclusively to customer needs and demands would be prohibitively expensive because the suppliers would have to adjust from the ground up to each new assignment and each new customer. What can be observed in many products is that rather than being tailored to the customer, they are not made the way they are because the customer wishes it, but because creating an economical and effective production process in the supplier company requires specific materials and manufacturing methods.

As a result, quality circles, continuous improvement processes, and kaizen initiatives are anchored primarily in the form of workshops. The reasons for this are strongly associated with the internal needs of consulting companies and quality assurance departments and relate less to the challenges facing their external and internal clients. For consulting firms and quality assurance departments, it is not only important that the internal or external customer is satisfied with the consulting services, but also that the consulting services can be provided without expending all too many internal resources. Thus, CIP and quality circles in one-hour meetings and kaizen in the form of workshops were very accommodating for consulting firms.

Providers of quality management services and consulting firms transformed the Japanese philosophy of quality into "ready-to-use" toolkits consisting of sequences of visuals, easily applied analytical tools, simple questioning techniques, standardized workshop concepts, and standards for conducting quality circle sessions that had been timed down to the minute. The ready-made toolkits—as research on quality circles has already recognized (Midler 1986)—resulted primarily from the consulting firms' interests in rapid growth.

I will illustrate the advantages of these ready-to-use toolkits using the highly standardized workshop concepts for quality circles, CIP, and kaizen. Irrespective of whether the quality initiatives were conducted under generic names or trademarked concepts such as Genesis, CEDAC, VIT or CIP2, in the companies under examination quality management structures were observed that were highly tailored to the needs of the consulting firms. There appeared to be a number of reasons for this.

First, standardized workshop concepts allowed the Japanese philosophy of quality to be anchored in Europe and America. The relevant quality management books by Japanese authors do not, phrasing it cautiously, shine based on their precision and concreteness. For example, if one takes a closer look at Masaaki Imai's book on kaizen, it is at first difficult to understand how businesses could have adopted the kaizen method based on this book. The author introduces kaizen in abstract terms as "change for the better" which is to be achieved through strict process and employee orientation and the ongoing improvement of set standards. In his writing, Imai vacillates between describing kaizen as a process, an attitude, a method, or a way of thinking—or perhaps all of the above. Significant portions of the book consist of impressively documented appeals that quality and change for the better are important and that permanent improvements should play a central role in corporations.

Consulting firms in Europe and America now appeared to face a challenge: kaizen was touted as the secret to success and was in great demand by corporations, but there was little concrete information on precisely how to implement it. If kaizen was presented as an employee orientation toward quality, productivity and permanent improvement, there was the problem that it was extremely difficult to anchor that kind of philosophy in a corporation. Attempts to establish a new way of thinking about quality through appeals to employees, glossy brochures, and motivational events are relatively blunt weapons in the struggle against quality problems, customer dissatisfaction, and production losses. Under these circumstances, the consultants resorted to the workshop as a form of organization.

Second, standardized workshops made it possible to use young, relatively inexperienced consultants. Particularly at the beginning of the boom in quality circles, CIP, and kaizen few seasoned experts were available. Young consultants had to be recruited and profitably deployed as quickly as possible. Workshops made this relatively simple. All the fledgling consultants had to learn was the quality ideology and the standard workshop procedures, and the client could be billed at a 4-figure per diem rate. Case in point, in one of the organizations studied recent university graduates could immediately be used as consultants because the high degree of standardization allowed a straightforward reproduction of the analytical tools, forms of intervention, and problem-solving mechanisms.

Third, by implementing kaizen, quality circles, and CIP in workshops, consulting firms could standardize their interventions to a large extent and thereby reduce internal costs. In an ideal case, the presentation and evaluation slides could remain virtually unchanged. Often, it was enough to replace the client's name on the slide. In the meantime, a number of CIP consulting firms work with standardized posters that can be used in a company completely irrespective of the specific nature of the problem.

Fourth, to conclude, highly standardized workshops enabled kaizen consultants to come into their clients' firms for a limited amount of time and yet still produce visible changes over a relatively short period. Photos of "before and after the workshop" could be used to demonstrate the obvious differences. This allowed the consultants to inform their clients that the investment in consulting services was quickly amortized. In the French firm, for example, photos were taken at regular intervals of the shop floor and storage areas after they had been reorganized, thereby demonstrating that hiring the consultants had been worth the money.

The Strengths and Weaknesses of a Workshop-Based Quality Concept

Even if accommodating the specific needs of consulting firms was the reason that various Japanese philosophies of quality were brought to Europe and America in the form of workshops, we must not overlook that they also appear to have produced a number of advantages for the corporations, government agencies, hospitals, and militaries that received the consulting services.

The testing of one-hour quality circles, continuous improvement processes, and kaizen workshops in various organizations created a relatively sophisticated and repeatedly revised concept. As a result, the client of a consulting firm enjoyed a relatively high degree of assurance with respect to the character of the quality process. Even at the beginning of a project, one could already envision relatively clearly the details of what was going to happen.

Furthermore, the frequent use of the same workshop concept generated a certain amount of pressure on organizations. Consultants could point out that Company A or Public Administration B in a neighboring community had been able to achieve a 30 percent productivity increase and a 50 percent reduction of throughput time using the very same workshop concept. This satisfied management's need to be certain that the investment in quality circles, kaizen, or CIP would pay off. All the same, it put corresponding pressure on the workforce to take the quality measures seriously.

In addition, the cost of the quality measures could be reduced. The organizations paid only for the implementation of the workshop, not for the development of the concept. In one case, the company refused to pay the consulting firm for the development of the workshop, citing the reason that the services received were of a standardized nature.

Nevertheless, focusing in part on the workshop character of the kaizen process also created problems. Due to the high degree of standardization, a workshop sometimes missed its target, namely, the organization's specific set of circumstances. In the facilities management firm, consultants applied kaizen principles that had been developed primarily for an assembly department. Due to the low degree of standardization entailed in maintenance work, however, the principles the consulting firm then presented were largely ineffective. In another company, the adaptation of the kaizen worksheets from previous projects was so approximate that even those responsible for kaizen inside the company did not know the exact meaning of the individual abbreviations.

A further problem is that concentrating on the workshop form initially caused employees to perceive kaizen as a surprise intervention from the outside. Some employees experienced it as a team of external and internal consultants, supported in part by a Japanese expert, "wafting" into their work area and explaining to the specialists on location which principles to use to reorganize the performance of their duties. It is understandable that something like that would occasionally generate considerable resistance.

Finally, in some cases focusing on workshops creates substantial problems for the sustainability of the kaizen process. The improvement measures that are implemented directly during the workshop itself are retained (some are also reversed) but improvement measures planned for the long-term grind to a halt amidst day-to-day business operations.

To a limited degree, such problems can be brought under control by changing (improving) the organization of the quality management process. Yet they do not change the underlying situation inasmuch as the character of the consulting services provided in quality management today tends to be shaped more by the internal needs of the consulting firms than the requirements of their clients.

4.5 Being Forced to Have Measurable Services: The Silent Spiral of Quality Management

Given the wide range of quality measures under discussion in organizations, critical voices repeatedly warn about constructing a "quality façade." Organizations that repeatedly proclaim new reorganization objectives in an inflationary way, it is claimed, will land themselves with a "Potemkin quality village" and run into difficulties with the corresponding "dual reality" it creates.

The Potemkin quality management façades are often viewed as an outcome of exaggerated efforts on the part of organizational leadership, contradictory and unrealistic management goals, or the defensive strategies of employees. Then, depending on the orientation of the observer, the approach to tearing down the façades is seen either in closer, more effective control of the quality measures taken by management, or a stronger employee orientation.

Criticism of the "Potemkin quality village" must not be limited to detecting the discrepancy between an organization's striving for quality and the dull reality of its day-to-day operations. Rather, it calls for reconstructing the strategies of individual players that lead to the formation of the quality façades in the organization's presentation, and an examination of the functionality of such façades for the organization overall.

The Tendency to Quantify the Successes of
Quality Management

"Only what is measurable is visible at all. Only measurable factors can be controlled and validated and therefore also improved." At the midsized firm of Veletto, this appeared to be the quality management motto. For all the quality tools, great value was placed on being able to quantify the results and measure employee commitment. In the framework of Veletto's company suggestion system, each employee was required to provide a certain number of improvement suggestions every year. Each individual suggestion was rewarded. In the quality circles, each of the trained internal moderators was required to conduct a certain number of workshops. For the kaizen measures, the effects of every individual workshop were calculated, and it was determined whether during the week in question the costs of the kaizen workshop were recovered through economies. For the Japan Diet, progress was quantified using the 20 keys and then made public.

The income of the laborers, master craftsman, and office workers at Veletto was linked to their performance in the quality management program. In addition to their salaries, employees could gain extra income through the premiums awarded under the company suggestion system. In the target agreement talks where salary increases were discussed, the CIP moderators were evaluated according to the number of workshops they had conducted. For executives, the Japan Diet was particularly relevant because their quantified performance in this quality initiative determined whether they received a bonus of up to 20 percent or, conversely, forfeited up to 10 percent of their pay.

The combination of quality management measures such as "quantifying the improvement suggestion program" and "rewarding participation" produced undesirable side effects. For example, employees submitted numerous suggestions, some of them pointless, for the sake of receiving additional bonuses. As one department head, put it, "Awarding bonuses across the board creates a lot of crap." In some instances, it was observed that individual employees would submit suggestions for improvement at times when they needed money for larger personal purchases. "I have one person," the department head continued, "who submitted 22-23 suggestions in January, and some of those improvements made absolutely no sense. Some people do it deliberately just to put money in their pockets."

Quality management assumes that company leadership will put an end to these universally well-known tricks. The assumption is based on the consideration that the higher employees are positioned in the hierarchy, the more they will identify with the organization's goal of making "quality products at favorable prices." Yet this overlooks that creating a façade of effective quality management can make good sense even for senior executives.

The façade character of quality management was not openly discussed in our midsize company because no one involved appeared to have an interest in turning the hype about their own quality and improvement system into a problem. The workers in manufacturing and assembly received bonuses for their improvement suggestions. Their superiors were required by their target agreements to meet a prescribed number of improvement measures, quality circles, and kaizen workshops, and could expect salary deductions and loss of face in the firm if they did not perform accordingly. The manager in charge of monitoring quality initiatives had allowed himself to be committed in his target agreement to a certain number of companywide suggestions and therefore often kept both eyes wide shut. Finally, Veletto's CEO was aware that having the company designated as the "factory of the year," which was his goal, depended on the number of suggestions for improvement, and therefore had no interest in exposing the inefficiency of the suggestion system that the employees had detected on the quiet.

Quality Managers, Consultants, and Team Leaders: Confederates in Myth

The CEO of Sommet, the French facilities management firm, was under considerable pressure to gain control of the quality deficit in the company's services. Customers had complained about it in a survey. As the manager of this business division, his intention was to use a broadly conceived kaizen initiative for all French teams as a way of signaling his superiors in the holding company that the quality problem was being tackled. Consequently, he established a task force consisting of seasoned staff members who were tasked with implementing the quality initiative in the various teams. The task force was required to report to the CEO at regular intervals. To support these internal employees, several consulting companies with kaizen credentials were hired. It was hoped that this would stimulate competition among the firms and thereby encourage greater commitment.

Externally, the kaizen initiative was always portrayed as a success that was also quantifiable. When the task force met with the CEO, long lists of improvements and calculations were presented, documenting that the savings produced by the kaizen initiative were exceeding its cost. As reported by a master craftsman, the pressure to succeed resulted in the performance of a "success show" at the end of each individual workshop. Since the results presented had to be quantifiable, a collective evaluation of the work steps saved, the storage areas cleared, and materials conserved was conducted on the last day of the workshop.

Nevertheless, the numbers reported were no more than loosely coupled with the results of the workshop. In part, the savings were quantified in areas where such quantification was impossible to undertake due to the complexity of the material. In such cases, one simply solicited an assessment from the team leader. Furthermore, successes the team had already achieved beforehand on its own were also attributed to the workshop. In isolated cases, outright pseudo-successes were presented. In one workshop, for example, a direct parking opportunity was designed for a large-scale facility in order to reduce unloading time for the laborers. Even though all of the participants knew that this created a solution only for the duration of the workshop—afterwards the facility once again involved long distances—for the success calculations at the end of the workshop savings for an entire year were calculated, to the amusement of the laborers concerned.

What was responsible for the exaggerated positive presentations of the workshop results? There was no deliberate collusion among the participants to massage the figures. Rather, the presentation of successes in the workshops was the result of tacit alliances, created under pressure and based on myths and fictions among the participating groups of players. The internal consultants were under pressure to document the efficiency of a measure in order to prove their own usefulness in a difficult situation, and possibly have additional personnel assigned to their task force. The external consultants were under pressure to chalk up quantifiable successes in their kaizen workshops in order to distinguish themselves against the other consulting firms. At one consulting firm, it was actually customary to link employees' pay to the savings achieved in their workshops. For the team and department heads in the firms that hired the consultants, the kaizen workshops provided an opportunity to present themselves as model teams or branch offices. This had been particularly encouraged because the CEO had called for increased internal competition between the teams and business areas, and promoted it with rankings, prizes, and commendations for their leaders.

From a Silent Circle to Spiraling Silence: The Escalation of Myth-Based Alliances

The myth- and fiction-based alliances that form around quality management do not represent organized conspiracies of employees at all hierarchical levels for the purpose of duping a customer who is striving for quality. Rather, they silently come into being due to the pressure of having to set up a comprehensive quality management program. They exist in a somewhat unconscious way as circles of silence. In such circles, interests that diverge from the quality ideology and the apparently paradoxical side effects of quality management can only be addressed to a limited degree. Although deviations from the supposedly fundamental principles of profitability, quality, and customer satisfaction may indeed arise frequently, the players cannot admit to them openly.

Not addressing the side effects, to paraphrase social scientist Elisabeth Noelle-Neumann, can lead to a "spiral of silence in quality management." Since the side effects are not openly discussed, management raises the target figures every year (the number of improvement suggestions, points on the Japan Diet scales, the number of CIP workshops, etc.). The employees react by expanding the scope of "Potemkin quality management" which, in turn, leads to further escalation of demands.

4.6 Quality Management Is the Answer, but What Was the Question, Actually?

If one reviews the current literature on quality management, pronounced end-means constructions become visible. Quality management is viewed as the central means to fulfill the supposed meta-goals of an organization, namely, securing one's livelihood and (as is often added from a labor union perspective) employee satisfaction. In the following step, quality management as a means is then defined as a sub-goal, and a wide range of means are utilized to achieve it, for example, quality circles, kaizen, or a company suggestion system. In turn, the latter are then set as goals, and means such as the use of standard instruments, employing consultants, and freeing up human resources are applied to achieve them.

As an example, in his quality planning concept pioneering American management thinker Josef M. Juran (Juran 1991, 168ff.) developed a hierarchical structure of quality ends or goals. From the top-level ends/goals he derives secondary ends and goals which then serve as fixed points for tertiary ends and goals. This results in pyramid shaped goal and sub-goal structures suggesting that the top-level goals can be achieved by gearing work strictly to the orders of ends and means.

Organizational research over the last 50 years has completely refuted the idea of clear end-means configurations. There is no doubt that they do exist and that the players have an interest in their sophisticated concatenation. The challenge is to the assumption that clear end-means chains even come close to allowing us to understand organizational processes. Instead, it is now assumed that the relationship between ends and means is significantly more complex. The implementation of quality management methods in day-to-day organizational reality is the very place this can be observed.

First, quality management is not a meta-goal toward which organizational activity would be oriented. In our example of the facilities management firm, there were the competing meta-goals of customer satisfaction and satisfying the holding company. Since these could not always be reconciled, informal structures emerged that allowed the processing of contradictory demands from the environment to go forward. The quality management program, which also addressed the informal processes, posed a danger for the organization inasmuch as the contradictory demands could no longer be processed informally as before.

Second, the use of means not only leads to the achievement of the desired goals but also creates a wide range of undesirable and paradoxical side effects. The blockade effect created when a number of different quality instruments are used, the recoil effect when quality management is linked to the Japan myth, and the limited perspective that results from the channeling of quality management efforts are examples of such undesired and paradoxical side effects.

Third, the means employed are not the only thing that results in the accomplishment of an intended goal; there are other, unplanned causes that contribute. While a number of factors which cannot be influenced may be responsible for an increase in revenues, customer satisfaction, or quality parameters, players who have vested interests frequently attribute them monocausally to a previously initiated quality management program. In the production of the "kaizen success" in the French company's workshops, the cause of certain effects was repeatedly traced to the kaizen method even though completely different reasons were responsible for the positive changes.

Fourth, it can be observed that goals are in part generalized to such a degree that they represent no more than abstract values. To state it in oversimplified terms, at the beginning of the quality management discussion one can observe a close linkage between quality and the supposed top-level goal of maximizing profit. An increase in quality that did not lead to increased profit would be rejected as irrational. In the current discussion, however, the usefulness of this means in terms of the top-level goal of increasing profit is in part no longer evident. Quality management is promoted because quality is a value in itself. In the midsized firm we studied, several employees expressed the suspicion that quality had in the meantime become a goal unto itself, independent of the goal of profit maximization.

In this context, we would like to mention a fifth point, namely, that goals change in conjunction with the means. Goals require and allow the use of certain means, the classical assumption runs. But as part of a recursive process, the availability of means also facilitates the emergence of new goals. Take computers as an example. It has been repeatedly shown that they are not only used as a means to achieve certain ends; their existence has also led to the formation of entirely new goals. Once a means has come into existence, the question arises of what other things one could use it for. In the case of our midsized firm, we observed that quality management as a means increasingly detached itself from the original goal of increasing profit, and a growing interest developed in using sophisticated quality management to win prizes for "business excellence." The goal change became so encompassing that critical voices were heard warning that one should not lose sight of the profit maximization motive.

For many years, the deconstruction of the instrumental-rational understanding of organizations was of interest exclusively to researchers in the field of organizational theory. An external description of organizations made it possible to examine aspects, development lines, and principles other than those which organizations were presenting in their self-descriptions. This divergence between external scientific description and practice-oriented self-description should not be construed as making a case for "correct" or "incorrect." Organizations certainly have many good reasons to promulgate an instrumental-rational model in their self-descriptions. Nevertheless, I think that even a practice-oriented discussion of quality management would receive important impulses through a greater focus on observing paradoxical and undesirable side effects and their integration into a more complex organizational model.

5.
Centralization through Decentralization

"Nobody is sure anymore who really runs the company
(not even the people who are credited with running it),
but the company does run."

Joseph Heller

In businesses, public administrations, and associations, the term "hierarchy" has unpleasant connotations. If one is to believe the scientific studies, in many organizations complaints about the undesired side effects of inadequate communication are part of everyday life. Apparently, employees at the top as well as those at the base complain that there is a type of information osmosis in the organization: much like semi-permeable membranes, hierarchical positions slowly diffuse information in one direction only, from the top to the bottom. Top management levels complain that this osmosis forces it to make important decisions based on unconfirmed information, because information filters up from the bottom reluctantly or in distorted form. The base, meanwhile, complains that the top echelons of the company do not consult it when decisions are made for which it has the corresponding professional know-how.

The reasons for this information osmosis in hierarchies were already worked out in the debate over Max Weber's concept of bureaucracy. Contrary to the classical premises of hierarchy theory, it has been shown that it is rarely possible to monopolize professional knowledge as well as external contacts at the top of the hierarchy. Due to the growing need for specialized know-how, subordinates often have greater expertise than their superiors. In addition, even positions located in the lower reaches of the hierarchy have their own external communications through which they obtain information that is relevant for the organization. As a result, superiors do not have at their disposal per se either the detailed expertise and knowledge of the environment or the good relationships of their subordinates to specific groups. Since all expertise and every contact with the environment cannot be reflected at the top, one also cannot expect the positions located at the top of a business's hierarchy to react to every change in the company's environment (for greater detail, see Luhmann 1971, 97ff.).

When decision-making competencies are centrally located at the top of a business, information that is relevant for decisions must be laboriously drawn up to the top from below. Yet even network studies from the 1950s showed that hierarchies are very rarely able to pull information upward against the flow of orders and sanctions. People who attempt to inform their superiors about a problematic situation expose themselves to the danger of being seen as the cause of the problem. Those who bear bad news risk being branded as culprits, and for that reason problematic information is often passed to higher levels only after it has been "doctored up" or not at all.

Instead of trying to perfect the flow of information from the bottom to the top, organizations are relying more and more on flattening hierarchies on the one hand, and decentralizing decision-making competencies on the other. While there is no logically compelling connection between the flattening of hierarchies and decentralization, most of the studies on new forms of business enterprises report that these two organizational strategies coincide.[7]

Research until now has pointed out two strategies for flattening hierarchies and decentralizing decision-making competencies in the

---

7   To simplify the matter, one can imagine a diagram with 4 fields: the one axis runs from "pronounced hierarchy" to "flat hierarchy," the other from "centralization" to "decentralization." Whereas the organizational model characterized by "pronounced hierarchy—centralization" corresponds to the ideal "classic" Taylorist organization, the model defined by "flat hierarchy—decentralization" is consonant with the ideal "new" form of organization. The two other possible organizational models in the 4-field diagram have until now been largely neglected by scientific research. An organization with a flattened hierarchy and centralized decision-making competencies would have to rely on strong standardization of decision-making programs and monitor compliance centrally through IT. In an organization with decentralized decision-making competencies and a pronounced hierarchy, one would expect "slack" to arise at the middle management level.

value-adding areas of an organization. The first entails a decentralization of responsibilities in parallel to removing entire levels of the hierarchy, thereby shortening lines of communication between top and bottom. This was researched in detail, particularly using major corporations such as GE, Siemens, or ABB as examples. It was found that although this strategy increases the span of control for superiors, the problem of too wide a range of contacts can be offset by decentralizing tasks to lower levels.

A second strategy for flattening a hierarchy involves no longer installing individual managers at the respective levels of the hierarchy, but forming teams and groups of members who have equal rights. This organizational principle has been analyzed in detail using assembly, production, and sales groups at the lowest hierarchical level. In spite of increased demands to expand the group principle to the executive level, until now there have been hardly any systematic studies of the transition from one-person leadership to leadership groups in the field of operative management.

In this chapter I will analyze how the introduction of leadership teams effects an organization. My thoughts are based on the observation of a company we will call Kontongo. Here, considerations on dehierarchization and decentralization were further radicalized, inasmuch as the company expanded the group work model from the production and assembly areas to the first management level by forming so-called leadership groups. Leadership groups are units that are formally equal teams and perform management duties relating to units below them in the hierarchy. The leadership group has no direct superior who can resolve conflicts based on formal authority. To the extent it is possible, conflicts are supposed to be resolved within the team through communication, negotiation, and coordination through discourse.

In the first part (5.1), I will analyze the motives that led to the expansion of the group principle from the value-adding level to the next higher levels. The second part (5.2) delineates four central organizational problems that arise through the introduction of team structures. Building on these considerations, part three (5.3) analyzes to what extent the goal of decentralizing competencies and responsibility can be achieved through the introduction of group work in the value-adding core and at the operative management level. In part 4 (5.4) and the concluding summary (5.5), I demonstrate that the very extensive form of decentralization created through the introduction of leadership teams actually creates a process that leads to the exact opposite, namely, a centralization of decision making.

5.1 The Concept of Managing as a Team: Expanding Group Work to the First Management Level

In the past, the concept of partially autonomous group work was applied almost exclusively to the lowest level of work organization, the immediate value-adding core. In experiments with teams in the context of programs to "humanize the workplace" during the 1970s and 80s, as well as in the operative decentralizations during the lean management wave of the 1990s, team structures without superiors were set up only at the level of direct value creation, which is to say, in the assembly and production areas of businesses, in the patient care areas of hospitals, or the service providing units of public administrations. At the first leadership level—the master craftsman, departmental, process line, or sector level—the principle of one-person leadership continued to be relied upon rather than the team leadership model.

Demands that one should no longer focus on the "one-man leadership model" but instead permit autonomy without the actual presence of a superior were implemented by executives almost exclusively for smaller project groups. Yet project groups have a completely different character than partially autonomous workgroups. Whereas the latter involve clearly defined work units with their own comprehensive tasks and a fixed place in the organizational chart, project teams form only on a temporary basis. The members of a project team, in addition to being part of the specific team, generally retain their ties to a department, sector, or executive position where they are integrated in a person-centered leadership structure.

Planning and Consulting Groups as a Team-Oriented Leadership Structure in Operative Management

Nevertheless, in practitioner literature on group work, we find the observation that the introduction of project teams and partially autonomous group work at the operative level of a company can only be a first step toward a flexible, learning organization. Trendy sounding organizational principles like "cellular organizations," "modular systems," or "agile businesses" are used to demand that the organizational structure of an enterprise should follow the "group principle" as much as possible, thereby creating an "organic group organization." The "basic groups"—which are called teams, partially autonomous groups, or tribes depending on the organization—are combined under the heading of "second-level groups." Following Rensis Likert (Likert 1961), there are demands that the superordinate leadership groups should primarily perform coordination and monitoring tasks, thereby placing all executive tasks in the hands of groups and no longer individuals.

The metaphor of a fractal organization is used to underscore the notion that leadership tasks should be transferred to groups and work teams to the greatest degree possible. According to this concept, all units of a business, association, or public administration are self-organized and self-similar in structure due to comprehensive team and group work. The assumption is that fractal enterprises, because of the special structure of their decentralized units, are better equipped to master the increasing complexity of day-to-day business operations. The idea is to facilitate coordination between the decentralized units by having all of the units function according to the same principles and thereby create a mutual understanding across all levels and areas of the organization. For example, the members of the board would be able to understand the problems of employees working together in groups because they themselves are organized in the form of group. Among employees, an understanding for the concerns of the company's leadership would arise because the employees act as quasi-entrepreneurs and can therefore relate to the thinking style of their "colleagues" in the top echelon.

Particularly in pioneering companies, a process of fermentation can be observed when it comes to the introduction of leadership groups at the master craftsman, departmental, and divisional levels. Transferring tasks such as job planning, resource planning, quality assurance, logistics, maintenance, and coordination to partially autonomous groups changes the tasks of the first leadership level. Instead of acting as technical experts, progress chasers, staffing planners, task allocators, and problem solvers as before, first level leadership is now called upon to perform tasks such as supporting self-governing groups, personnel development, promoting collaboration in groups, planning the qualification process, and providing assistance with relaunch projects.

In light of this shift in tasks at the first leadership level, companies, and especially their consultants, raise the question of why the leadership tasks are not also performed by groups, instead of individuals. Particularly in the dominant thread of labor science literature on group work, there are calls for the introduction of planning and advisory teams at the first management level which, jointly and without formal superiors, are supposed to assume the tasks of strategic planning, production program planning, materials management, quality planning, and operations scheduling.

The Reasons for the Introduction of Team Structures

Kontongo implemented the idea of planning and advisory groups at the first management level and thereby assumed a pioneering role in the European, American, and Japanese automobile industry. The overall framework was to split the company into five sectors, but rather than installing classical one-person leadership for each, responsibility for the respective sectors was transferred to a team. Personnel and organizational development viewed the creation of leadership/sector teams as an "extension of teams to the next hierarchical level." The "traditional master craftsman function" was to be integrated into a holistic leadership team.

The sector teams were composed of master craftsmen from production and engineers from the engineering departments, in other words, people who had been active in different areas until that time. The teams consisted of 4–6 employees. Team members were supposed to assume the jobs of process engineering, personnel support, materials management, and information management, as well as responsibility for the budget and quality assurance. The sector team was in charge of the budget and was authorized to purchase several million euros worth of spare parts, lubricants, auxiliary supplies, and maintenance services. Every employee in the sector team was assigned a primary duty, but was also supposed to be able to stand in for other members.

All members of the team were coequal and had the same authority over subordinate groups. Just as in the production and assembly groups, the leadership team also had a spokesperson who was supposed to act as a contact person to plant management and assume a coordinating function in the sector team. The sector spokesperson did not have disciplinary authority over the other members of the leadership team. The corporate development officer of Kontongo explains: "The sector spokesperson can be compared to the group spokesperson in the assembly and production islands. That means, the job is truly supposed to be that of a speaker who acts as an intermediary between individual positions."

Management hoped that establishing coequal leadership groups would produce synergy effects, increase the exchange of experience among employees, and encourage flexibility through mutual assistance and substituting for one another. In particular, the inclusion of engineers in the leadership groups was intended to stimulate a transfer of know-how on location, which would then lead to faster and more direct problem solving.

By setting up leadership teams, Kontongo's top management wanted to overcome the problems of functional differentiation in the organization. The original idea underpinning functional differentiation was to break down the organization's overall objective into individual tasks, each of which could be accomplished through separate, highly professionalized departments. From the perspective of top management, however, the difficulty of this strategy was that departments such as quality assurance, construction, and production dedicate themselves to perfecting their respective local rationalities. On this basis, specific interests of the individual divisions subsequently emerged which stood substantially in contradiction to one another. Frequently, the only way to reconcile such particular interests is to weigh one against the other at the highest level of the organization and resolve the inter-departmental conflicts there as well. In such cases, the hierarchy functions as a specialized agency for coordinating what was previously differentiated.

In the company under examination, management hoped that by creating leadership teams the problems resulting from specific interests would be brought together in one place where they could be solved through compromise, communication, and consensus. The expectation was that the top echelon of the company would no longer be burdened with rectifying internal conflicts. Groups with heterogeneous compositions in particular would be able to reproduce the complexity of a sector's relevant environments better than groups that were dominated by an executive, and it was hoped that this would offer advantages. The leadership groups were intended to introduce fuzziness where individuals, based on their professional logic or their affiliation with a specific department, resorted to either-or simplifications. In this manner, the ambivalence and discrepancies inherent in an organization were to be turned into a resource that would open up the sectors to a range of rationales. Carrying out conflicts in the leadership teams was supposed to prevent problematical simplifications and contribute to finding more appropriate solutions.

5.2 The Problems of Collaborating in Teams

In labor science, a controversial debate is underway as to why it is so very difficult to introduce group and team-oriented structures. Although one might expect that the employees affected would welcome this new form of work due to its humanizing potential, one observes instead that, in part, the employees who are to be organized in groups and teams put up resistance.

For many years, the resistance was explained through the psychology of learning: it was insinuated that the employees would actually like to become involved with this new form of work, but were not yet able to because of defensive routines. Later, explanations gained traction which, following Pierre Bourdieu, attributed the resistance to the introduction of a bourgeois work habitus into the fields of production and assembly that were characterized by a proletarian concept of work. For example, ethnologist Andreas Wittel (Wittel 1998) argued that while collaboration in groups, with its emphasis on intrinsically motivated and discursively oriented work, encourages the formation of a bourgeois habitus, laborers resist it because they have been shaped by a concept of work that is oriented toward earning, physicality, subordination, and routine.

This line of argumentation enriched the discussion of the problems and resistance created through the introduction of group work with an additional cultural-sociological explanation. Nevertheless, it suggests that it would be easier to introduce group and team structures in the areas of a business, public administration, or hospital that are not characterized by a proletarian work habitus, and that it would not encounter the same resistance and problems. According to this reasoning, introducing team structures at leadership levels, where an intrinsically motivated and discursively oriented work habitus has always played an important role, should be easier to accomplish than in the operative areas. But do the problems with group work really diminish the more we have to do with employees who have higher qualifications, are better paid, and more articulate?

In the following section we will use four problem areas to examine in greater detail the difficulties of workgroups on the one side and leadership groups on the other.

The Problem of Decision Making under the Consensus Principle

The need to make fast, accurate decisions under "turbulent conditions" is a key argument in favor of the introduction of group work, segmentation, and the flattening of hierarchies. Henry Mintzberg (Mintzberg

1979, 183), for example, justifies dehierarchization and decentralization measures by pointing out the opportunity they provide to react quickly to local conditions. Transferring information back and forth from a branch office to headquarters takes time which businesses simply no longer have in today's environment.

From the perspective of the employees at Kontongo, however, the advantages of introducing group structures at the operative and the leadership levels only became apparent when a decision could be taken "in peace." In contrast, the dismantling of hierarchical authority structures emerged as a problem when decisions were made under time pressure, which is to say, the very situations in which decentralized organizational structures are assumed to offer an advantage. According to the head of the assembly department, "Under overload conditions, group work tends to get in the way. You're better off with clear instructions. Because you just can't keep talking about things for hours or days. A heavy workload tends to have a negative effect on group work."

In a classical organizational structure, the hierarchically legitimized instructions of a previously defined person in charge allow decisions to be reached quickly. Since there is no one who is authorized to issue instructions, either at the level of group work or in leadership teams, consensus-oriented mechanisms for reaching agreement become more important. The necessity and the opportunities for communication in the teams intensifies. In the process, the "communication load" increases rapidly as the number of team members grows.

The employees in the groups find themselves in a communications dilemma. They must rely on routine, scheduled communication because it is difficult for them to assess what must be agreed upon and what information needs to be supplied. At the same time, a sense of communication overload arises. One member of a leadership team at Kontongo complained, "I can't be forever trying to inform myself what the other people in the segment team are doing at any moment. There's simply too much duplication of effort. There's a lot of talk, and that leads to the exchange of information, but we're also blocking each other's resources. The duplication of work is caused by imprecise definitions or the incomplete implementation of precise definitions." In this dilemma, the team members inclined toward laborious voting processes because they didn't want to risk that one of their colleagues, with whom they worked together every day, felt left out.

Particularly when questions are controversial, a decision cannot be reached even in extreme situations, because there is no entity in the group who has the final say. This causes decision-making pressure so intense that one puts up with the serious psychological stress and ultimately reaches a decision—although sometimes the groups have no option but to leave the decision to a superior. One member of a leadership team facing a problematical decision reported, "In spite of the lack of time, progress was made because the people up above intervened with guidance—at our request, because as a group of six we can't take a vote on everything. If you do that, you can't make any decisions at all, it takes too long."

It is interesting that the problem of reaching decisions quickly existed in very similar form in the production and assembly groups as well as the leadership groups. The higher qualifications and greater discursive orientation of the members of the sector team therefore did not appear to guarantee that consensual agreement functioned any better in this group than in the production and assembly groups. On the contrary, there are indications that the problem arises even more frequently and intensely in leadership groups, because their tasks are less standardized in comparison to those of the production and assembly groups.

Moreover, the introduction of group structures aggravates the time problem when a decision is reached only after the next higher level of the organization has been involved. It can happen that a problem will remain in a production or assembly group for a long time, where a decision based on the consensus principle cannot be reached, and is then handed up to a leadership team because a deadline is in danger. Since the nature of the problem often involves conflict and discrepancies, the problematical decision now reproduces itself in the leadership team, which is burdened with an extremely time-consuming decision-making process.

The Diffusion of Responsibility

A frequently mentioned problem of classical one-person management is that responsibility lies with a single individual, and the other employees do not feel accountable for the performance of the team. To prevent this, in group work the responsibility for quality, productivity, and adherence to schedule is no longer assigned to one individual but to the group overall. As an example, the personnel development officer at Kontongo remarked, "For the sectors, there is one uniform job description. Allocating the numerous duties is then up to the members themselves." The members also had to be able to stand in for one another. Each of them had to be independently able to order supplies and parts, conduct conversations with employees, and schedule shifts and vacations.

Nevertheless, contrary to the expectation that team leadership in the sectors would lead to greater acceptance of responsibility, a greater diffusion of responsibility was observed in the company under examination. Particularly at the plant management level, complaints were voiced that the sector teams were not assuming responsibility for quality, production, and adherence to schedule in a form that was appropriate for a sector structure. For example, in the question of vacation planning—which was actually a task of the production and assembly groups themselves—the decisions which ultimately applied were not even reached at the level of the leadership team. Here, the problems for which the members of the leadership team dodged responsibility were formulated in such a way that they could no longer be seen as the duty of the leadership team, but were viewed instead as a cross-functional task. The formulations conveyed the impression that the leadership team was no longer responsible. In the words of the head of production, "On the one hand, they don't have the confidence to make the decision, so they pass it up to a higher level. The submissions are phrased like this: we in the sector team are not able to make this decision, we don't have permission to do so."

The members of the leadership team justified their rejection of responsibility by saying that taking too prominent a stance would ultimately result in a person becoming the scapegoat for every problem that arose. "Here's the way it is in our company," one member of the leadership team remarked. "Once somebody's been held responsible, then that's the only person they always beat up on, to put it bluntly." That was particularly problematical when one had no hierarchically anchored authority over one's colleagues. When it came to the spokespeople, one had the impression that they had to put their neck on the line for certain things even though they did not bear sole responsibility for them.

In this respect as well, it was emphasized that in the assembly and production islands the problem of the diffusion of responsibility did not arise with the same stridency as in the leadership teams. The assigned task, according to the head of production, "keep the group on track." In contrast, the tasks of managers were burdened with much greater insecurity factors, which tended to make standardization difficult. In the team structures at the middle management level, this apparently provided more room for games involving the acceptance and rejection of responsibility than in the fields of operative activities.

In leadership teams, the diffusion of responsibility escalated to a point where, contrary to the recommendation of plant management, no sector spokesperson was appointed. As justification, the teams fielded the argument that responsibility for the work rested on the entire sector. "If we're a sector," said one member of a team that was particularly at loggerheads, "then that means four, five, or six of us. Because the executives at the top were planning, if there are problems, to single out just the sector spokesperson and solve the problem with him, or hold one individual responsible for not solving the problem."

Employees Play One Member of the Leadership Team against the Other

Management hoped that the introduction of team-oriented leadership structures would allow it to present itself to employees in a clear, coordinated fashion. The classical strategy of the production and assembly workers was to pit executives from operations scheduling, quality management, construction, and job controlling, who were located in different departments, one against the other. Management calculated that this could be counteracted by combining the executives from the various departments into a leadership team with shared responsibility.

When there was no time pressure, the sector team actually did present a unified, consolidated front to the employees. Yet contrary to management expectations, under stressful conditions the introduction of sector teams did not result in clear and coordinated behavior of the sector team toward production and assembly workers. As a result of combining representatives from operations scheduling, quality management, construction, and job controlling into one team with shared responsibility, there was no longer a clear contact person even for technical questions. The employees therefore had the impression that there was no longer a clear line in the sectors. As one assembly worker remarked about his leadership team, "They're constantly changing their tune, because now communication in the sector is not clearly defined."

The poorly delineated responsibilities gave the partners of the sector teams an opportunity to play one member against the other. This tendency could be observed in the relationship between the leadership team and the work groups as well as the relationship between the leadership team and the job controlling department. For example, the controllers from the order processing center tried to pit the members of the sector teams against one another. Each of the seven job controllers tried to sway the members of the sector team to treat his own specific jobs preferentially. If he was unsuccessful with one team member, he would move on to the next, thereby exploiting communication gaps in the leadership team for his own ends.

Particularly the subordinates of the leadership teams developed sophisticated strategies to profit from the unclear allocation of responsibilities. As the personnel development officer remarked, "Often, the group doesn't know who the contact person is, because that's also not really communicated externally. So, then the members of the group try to push through their personal interests and play games." And a member of the leadership team commented, "When people in the leadership team aren't talking with one another, then your own people turn out to be really filthy characters. If I tell someone, 'You can't do that,' he'll move on to the next person; so, something's already gone wrong." Attempts to prevent the employees' games by increasing communication between them were not always successful in day-to-day business operations. A member of the sector team told us, "The members of the groups have already realized that you can play one member of the sector team against the other. They look for the path of least resistance, and we prevent that by coming to an agreement among ourselves. Vacations and comp time is the only area where some people succeed in getting a vacation day by talking to the right person."

Power Struggles in Leadership Groups

The hope behind introducing group and teamwork is to achieve better cooperation and communication among employees. The idea is to provide employees a home and security in the group by creating circles of people that remain as constant as possible and can perform their duties independently to a large degree. The group structure is meant to reduce internal conflicts, and conflict potential is supposed to be diverted to external "enemies."

Empirical research on lateral cooperation in businesses nourishes this hope. Lateral cooperation is defined as the "goal-oriented fulfillment of cross-functional tasks, based on the division of labor and in a structured work situation, by members of an organization who are formally or approximately equal in terms of the hierarchy." In its observations of people on the same hierarchical level, quantitative research on lateral cooperation has found that employees have more than twice as many conflicts with individuals outside of their group as inside. This suggests that cooperation inside the same department functions better than cooperation between employees of different departments.

In contrast to that, research from an industrial sociological and systems theoretical perspective has found that the principle of self-organization does not completely eliminate power struggles; on the contrary, they now become especially relevant. Self-organization hampers the establishment of structured authority. The distribution of power becomes more diffuse for everyone involved, and it becomes very difficult for individual members of the group to defend themselves against misuse of the power structure. Technical problems quickly become overlaid with personal antipathies. As one sector team reported, "Punches were being thrown below the belt."

The power struggles tended to be personal and were explained through the absence of a superior. One member of a leadership team at Kontongo remarked, "If there were a superior, a formal sector leader, we wouldn't have these interpersonal problems, because then there would be a boss." In other words, in operative management superiors were not seen exclusively as a hindrance by any means. Instead, they were also viewed as protecting employees from escalating internal group conflicts.

In the production and assembly groups, the orientation toward clearly defined tasks allowed us to observe an informal regulating mechanism that could not arise in leadership teams in the same form. The "Darwinist power struggle" seen in workgroups that had no superior resulted in the development of pecking orders based on the criterion of performance. Influence and status in the group depended to a large degree on mastering tasks and were therefore relatively easy for members to determine. If a person could not perform the task required, others in the group took note and the respective individual was sanctioned. As a final consequence, members who did not perform, thereby reducing the bonus payments for the entire group, were removed. Case in point, a group speaker in the assembly department at Kontongo reported, "There was one person where there were documented quality problems, so then the group wouldn't put up with that anymore."

The reason that leadership teams have so few options for regulating internal power struggles is related to the fact that, in principle, they have no standardized tasks. Even early research on the rationalization of work in the service sector pointed out that tasks in the support areas of a business are characterized by a high degree of technical, time, personnel, and economic indeterminacy (Berger 1984). As a result, it is difficult for informal pecking orders to arise in leadership teams. The corporate development officer at Kontongo compared the situation in a particularly problematic leadership team to Monty Python's *Silly Olympiad*: "Everyone was running in a different direction." In terms of their contributions to adding value, leadership, engineering, and support tasks cannot be precisely defined, which made it impossible for the sector team to form a group consensus on the performance of individual members. In this sense, resorting to the supposed authority of experts is a means of exerting power that is strongly defined by subjective impressions. The option of regulating or reducing a conflict by evaluating a member's performance does not exist.

The structural problem arising from the difficulty of determining performance is exacerbated because executives have a different motivational structure. A member of the sector team remarked, "Far too much energy is wasted … on ranking in the company." According to the corporate development officer, for example, executives were not only motivated by money, but had a strong interest in advancing their careers and receiving recognition by their superiors. Meanwhile, in decentralized structures the chances of advancing in middle management are extremely limited because there are hardly any opportunities to do so. If one wanted to have any kind of career at all, the corporate development officer stated, when opportunities for advancement are limited it was important to be "identifiable as a person." The only way to have a career was to be perceived as an individual and not as a team member. A sector team member at Kontongo told us, "I see my boss twice a month, and then only if he comes down here … Then there are people who can't stand that, so they have to run and see the boss three or four times a month. And then false information is spread; you have absolutely no idea."

When the plant manager was brought into the escalating conflicts as the top executive, the result was often nothing more than a further exacerbation of the conflict because he had hardly any knowledge of the detailed processes in the sectors and could therefore be used by various team members for their own purposes. As the personnel development officer at Kontongo remarked, "Many times, the respective higher-level executives can't make that judgment ... because they don't know what's going on in the sectors. There are a lot of opportunities to scheme and do something nasty to a colleague."

The Blind Spots in Team Leadership

In part, the above-mentioned difficulties can surely be traced to problems caused by establishing a new, unfamiliar leadership structure. Those who were promoting it expressed the hope that informal regulating mechanisms would evolve in the leadership groups that would mitigate the problems observed up to that point. Nevertheless, it would be a mistake to trace all of the problems of team and group organization—in the style of the sometimes euphoric literature on group work—exclusively to its introduction or the lack of team-oriented socialization in employees. In the four problems discussed above, it was instead a question of the "blind spots" that are created when group work is used to achieve greater flexibility.

The problems described above represent the other side of the coin. They arise at exactly the points where an attempt is made to use group work to escape the negative effects of Taylorist work organization. If one intends to increase the quality of decisions by grouping players with divergent interests together and pressuring them to achieve a consensus, then one has to accept the problematical nature of decisions that have been reached quickly. Strengthening a sense of responsibility by holding entire groups responsible, as opposed to a single individual, entails the risk of diffusing responsibility. The effect that the members of teams pit themselves against one another is understandable if the object is to make a number of contact people available and thereby achieve the most seamless support possible for upstream and downstream areas. True, conflicts and power struggles can be painful for individual employees, but they must be accepted if one combines once functionally differentiated areas of responsibility in a team, and views conflicts as an opportunity to expand the organization's spectrum of awareness.

Comparing production or assembly groups with leadership groups provides clear indications that the difficulties encountered in group work have less to do with the cultural characteristics of production and assembly workers, than with the specific conditions created by the process of reaching decisions without a superior. The problems and resistance that arise on the operative leadership level with respect to group and team structures seem very similar to those in the immediate, value-adding core.

Due to the different position of executives in an organization, the problems of group structures arise in part even more stridently than in teams in value-adding departments. First, the high degree of task standardization in the production and assembly groups, and the existence of clear programs and specifications, can partially prevent the escalation of problems entailed in consensual decision making. In contrast, the spectrum of responsibilities in leadership teams is far less standardized, and the criteria available to mitigate discursive decision-making processes are therefore less clearly defined. Second, since middle management is sandwiched between top management above and the value-adding areas below, power, control, and responsibility games can be played in two directions—and not just unidirectionally as in assembly and production teams.

Building on the structural problems of team decision making elucidated here, the next section will discuss the paradoxical effects that can arise when two serially connected levels of the hierarchy are based on group structures instead of one-person leadership.

5.3 The Decentralization Paradox: Team Leadership and the Centralization of Decision Making

As a rule, one assumes that flattening hierarchies and introducing group and team structures on all levels of a business will result in greater decentralization of responsibility. Granted, there are isolated cases of organizations attempting to reduce their hierarchies without decentralizing decision-making authority. In most businesses the maxim would appear to be: the greater the flattening of the hierarchy and the more pronounced the decentralization efforts, the more competencies and responsibility are shifted downward. There is talk of the "cascade effect of decentralization." Mid-level managers who have received greater responsibility and authority in flatter hierarchies can only survive if they themselves, in turn, cede authority and responsibility to levels underneath them.

At first sight, the assumption seems convincing. At Kontongo as well, management assumed that flattening the hierarchy, introducing team structures on various levels, and decentralizing responsibility would also lead to better decision making at the two lowest levels of the hierarchy. In the following, I will analyze why the desired effect materialized only to a limited degree.

Opportunities to Exert Hierarchical Authority in Team-Oriented Leadership Structures

Hierarchical positions that are filled by individuals have a central function in organizations. They are crystallization points for decision-making authority, and they are points at which flows of communication and information are interrupted. The interruption function of the hierarchy works in both directions. Not all information in an organization is transferred from the bottom to the top because this would completely overwhelm the uppermost echelon. Likewise, not all information is passed down from the top to the operative area, the technical core, via the middle management level. The task of middle management lies in filtering information from superiors according to its relevance and then passing only some of it along.

The interruption function allows organizations to process a high degree of complexity. In the thinking of Herbert A. Simon (Simon 1965), it is a central function of hierarchy to produce a series of interlocking systems and subsystems. Simon claimed that, as a rule, communication is stronger and more intense within the individual systems and subsystems than between them. There is greater communication within a department than between departments; the exchange of ideas within a group is more intense than between groups. In this manner, a modular system of partially autonomous units arises where complete partial solutions can be worked out. It is only at the end that these must be combined into a total solution. And when new tasks arise, one can selectively refer back to them.

Linking their units in pyramidal chains of command is what makes it possible for organizations to communicate in a consistent fashion to begin with. According to the thinking of Niklas Luhmann (Luhmann 1997, 834), in the absence of a time-consuming (and impossible) creation of consensual agreement among all employees, the sole reason an organization can speak with one voice is that a CEO, chairman of the board, or mayor can depend on his instructions being implemented as concrete actions in semi-autonomous modules via the hierarchical pyramid.

At Kontongo, over the course of decentralization measures the old master craftsmen-based structures were removed; the "kingdoms" of the master craftsmen were abolished. Yet the master craftsmen and the decision-making authority so closely associated with them as individuals had fulfilled an important function for the interruption of communication in the company. There is another side to complaints about the paralyzing, deadwood echelons of middle management in business operations, namely, that the managers with their extensive competencies were very effectively able to secure the functioning of the company's modular structure. Casting it in positive terms, a master craftsman in the company under discussion was previously able to relieve the pressure put on his superiors by information coming from his unit, but he also filtered information from his superiors for its relevance to levels below.

The introduction of team structures at the first management level resulted in a modification of the information filtering structures. When day-to-day operations were functioning, there was no great difference to the previously existing master craftsmen structure. Since sufficient time was available to reach consensual decisions on the leadership group level, decisions could be reached at that point as to which information would be passed along to employees in the form of instructions or suggestions. Information could move through the official channels.

In time-critical situations—for example, when complaints were filed or rush jobs had to be inserted into the production stream—the function of leadership teams as filters from higher to lower levels was limited. The large span of control and the often tedious process of reaching agreement in the team made it increasingly difficult for production management to gain access to employees "by the book." The regular procedure—plant management turns to sector team, sector team reaches an agreement and then passes information along to the groups, the groups reach an agreement and speak to individual employees—was perceived as extremely time-consuming by the head of production and was often overridden.

Thus, particularly in critical moments the sector team was bypassed and direct drastic measures were taken. The director of total quality management at Kontongo reported, "The head of production intervened in the group externally without discussing it beforehand." The personnel development officer concurred, "That actually happens very often. When something happens that requires immediate action, then the boss becomes personally involved. Meanwhile, when the direction is from the bottom to the top, they usually stick to the 'official channels.'" From the perspective of the sector team, the agreed-upon division of tasks was rarely upheld. A member of the sector team remarked, "The managers don't care about the internal job descriptions. Even though they are aware of them, if there's a problem, more often than not they'll pick out the next best person in the sector team, even if the person has no responsibility for it at all."

Here, it can be seen plainly how the loose linkage that was introduced through team structures was perceived by those affected as a source of stress to which they reacted with tight linkage. Organizational psychologist Karl Weick (Weick 1976) pointed out early on that loose linkage in organizations can result in a sudden conservation of structures because hierarchies, due to the problems created by all-too-loose linkage, suddenly remobilize classical chains of command. The decentralization produced by group structure on a number of levels gives the head of production the ability to access production employees directly to a much greater degree than under the previous master craftsmen-based structure.

Hierarchy as a Stop Rule for Idling in Group Decision Making

Parallel to the head of production's ability to override the weak level of middle managers who have been organized into a team, the paradox of centralization through decentralization also manifested as a result of initiatives from below. At Kontongo, we observed that a decentralization of decision-making competencies also occurred when the teams had sufficient time to reach their decisions, when the problem did not mobilize overly controversial positions in the team, and informal hierarchization, divisions of labor, or coordination processes formed. Nevertheless, particularly when the decisions were time critical and were handled by groups where the distribution of power had not been clarified through informal negotiations, the decentralization of decision-making authority did not work. Since decisions in groups could not be made based on authority of office, when conflict arose decisions were passed upward in the hierarchy until they reached a person who had a decision-making monopoly.

In such cases, we noticed that, paradoxically, all of the measures directed at decentralization or dehierarchization and all of the changeovers from hierarchical to discursive management took place within the framework of a hierarchy that remained in force. In unproblematic situations, the underlying existence of a fundamentally hierarchical organizational structure is often difficult to perceive in strongly decentralized organizations. It is obscured by management's talk of democratization, empowerment, and dehierarchization. In moments of crisis, however, the basically hierarchical structure becomes virulent: decisions relating to terminations, salary cuts, or increased work hours are not reached through consensus, but are suddenly based on precedence of rank.

When decision-making processes were going nowhere, or problems were time critical and groups did not reach consensus immediately, in the organization under discussion the head of production represented the first level where conflicts could be decided through a vote. This was because it was the first level where responsibility was concentrated in one person. According to a member of the sector team, "The only way you can resolve the conflict is to take it to the boss." As an example, in one team problems related to the allocation of tasks were reported that could only be resolved through an intervention by the head of production. The question concerned which team member was allowed to perform which tasks, and how responsibilities would be allocated. Since the debate also involved the question of who would have what kind of influence in the future, the team had a falling out and could not reach a consensus. As a member of the sector team told us, "First we tried it on our own. That wasn't so great. Then we took it to HR, and that didn't work either. So, then we went to the plant manager, and that was very effective."

It is considered a strength of hierarchies that they can call a stop to negotiation processes or "pull the emergency brake." They ensure that solutions to problems can be found. Even Max Weber (Weber 1976, 561) emphasized that bureaucracies, because of their unequivocal decision-making programming through record-keeping and official instructions, as well as their tight principle of super- and subordination, had prevailed over collegial, volunteer, and adjunct forms of organization. Precision, speed, unambiguity, and continuity, the central characteristics of an organization, could only develop due to a combination of programming and hierarchy.

Systems theory in particular presents a variation on this thought by pointing out that from a functional perspective, hierarchy makes it possible to transform an infinite information load into a finite one. The stop rules or emergency brakes are constructed in such a way that when a process that normally occurs through discursive coordination encounters a crisis, the hierarchy is mobilized. Dirk Baecker (Baecker 1999, 298ff./330ff.) states that employees in modern organizations are in a position that makes them experts in a highly sensitive intermediate step, and thereby forces them to check back in every halfway demanding task. The hierarchical stop rule or emergency brake suspends this very principle of being able to check back. The hierarchy derives its legitimation from itself; it is not required to justify itself by referring to technical knowledge, contacts in the environment, or inspiration.

As a rule, the new organizational hierarchies are constructed in such a way that following each level with group or team structures there is a level with unequivocal personal assignment of responsibility. Following the level of partially autonomous assembly and production islands comes the level of the master craftsman who bears personal responsibility. Following the level of a coequal management team in the leadership of a profit center comes a board member who bears personal responsibility. Situated above a project team with coequal members, there is a project leader who can make decisions about problems in the project team by referring to her position. In this manner, a hierarchy can very quickly contain the undesired paradoxical effects of group and team structures.

In contrast to this, at Kontongo the hierarchical stop rule was only triggered close to the top. The employees spoke of a "broken organization." The production levels with the two team and group structures, building one upon the other, were strongly decentralized and got along with a very flat hierarchy, but the rest of the business organization continued to function according to strict, hierarchical principles. At the interface between the decentralized and the classical, hierarchical organization based on one-person leadership—which is to say, in the function of the production or plant manager—problems occurred that could not be decided using the team structures because there was no single person with clear responsibility. When decisions were time critical, the topics highly adversarial, and the team situations problematic, it could happen that, due to the late triggering of the hierarchical stop rule, problems stemming from the production and assembly groups were not solved until they reached the production management level.

We can speak of a paradox because the existence of two levels with group and team structures built one upon the other has the effect that decisions are reached in an even more centralistic manner than if a classical master craftsmen structure were in place, where a master craftsman was able to shorten a decision-making process by referring to his hierarchical competencies. When groups are unable to regulate conflict through informal hierarchization, the division of labor, or by reaching a consensus, particularly in such pronounced decentralized structures, decisions are moved up to a higher level in the hierarchical pyramid. The outcome is that critical problems gather at one point in the organization, namely, a single individual, in a process that Henry Mintzberg (Mintzberg 1979, 385f.) refers to as "centralization."

The Erosion of Decentralized Decision-Making Structures

In summary, it can be said that in stress situations the establishment of group structures across two hierarchical levels can lead to an erosion of the planned decentralization of decision-making processes. Organizational practice deviates from the intended and agreed-upon decentralized approach. It was striking that neither the members of the production and assembly groups, the members of the management group, or plant management appeared in principle to be interested in recentralizing decision-making competencies. Moving decisions upward when organizational stress situations arose was recognized by everyone affected as a procedure that increased complexity unnecessarily, but paradoxically was almost unpreventable.

One could view the deviation from the agreed-upon decentralized decision-making structures as a necessary and, for the organization, functional infraction of the rules. Infractions that are practiced in a contained manner can actually contribute to adherence to the regulations because situations and contexts in which the rules do not appear to be applicable do not immediately result in delegitimization of the rules overall.

Under the circumstances described, however, the result appears to be a self-reinforcing circle where decentralized decision-making structures erode more and more. Deviations from the intended and agreed-upon rule that "decisions are to be made in groups" are so frequent that escalating problematic decisions up to a higher level increasingly threaten to become a dominant organizational practice. Because the hierarchy is flat, more and more decisions need to be reached by the plant manager who thereby becomes the eye of the needle for time critical and controversial decisions.

The following considerations will integrate the proposition as developed until now into two central threads of the decentralization discussion.

5.4 Variations on Centralized Decentralization: Consequences for the Discussion of New Forms of Organization

There are two discussion threads that are important for defining the observations that have been made. The first consists of the attempt to elaborate the simultaneity of decentralization and centralization strategies—rather than simply juxtaposing them—and thereby to define more precisely the proportions of the mixture of centralization and decentralization. The second discussion thread attempts to point out in greater detail the undesired ancillary consequences, paradoxical effects, and dilemmas that decentralization and dehierarchization efforts produce.

In the following, I would like to draw on the empirical results presented in the previous sections and the theoretical considerations I developed there. This will connect the two discussion threads which, until now, have tended to run parallel to one another. In the new post-bureaucratic forms of organizations, not only do identity conflicts, politicization problems, and explosions of complexity arise as undesired but unavoidable costs of a more flexible organizational structure, under certain circumstances decentralization strategies can actually accomplish the very opposite of what was originally intended.

Centralized Decentralization as a Management Strategy

The postmodern sounding replacement of the either-or principle with the as-well-as principle has also found its way into the management debate. Whereas it initially looked as if deciding between decentralization *or* centralization involved the question of creating clearer, cleaner conditions in an organization, it is now increasingly argued that organizations pursue decentralization *as well as* centralization strategies simultaneously. A number of studies on decentralization have defined more closely the apparently paradoxical relationship between centralization and decentralization, and it has been brought to light that management attempts to exploit the advantages of decentralized, self-organization, at the same time that it utilizes the synergy effects of centralized governance.

Alfred Kieser (Kieser 1994, 219f.) elaborated that it would be an illusion to believe that external organization would be dialed back for the purpose of promoting self-organization. Rather than making a blanket assumption of "self-organization instead of external organization," he suggests focusing greater attention on the "external organization of self-coordination and self-structuring." This opens up the perspective that it is only external organization that makes self-coordination in decentralized units possible in the first place. Seen from different theoretical perspectives, various combinations of external organization and self-organization, that is, centralization and decentralization, suggest themselves.

An initial line of argumentation in the tradition of control theory points out that, contrary to post-Fordian assumptions, decentralization does not lead to a strengthening of small, autonomous units. Instead, control is concentrated to a much greater degree in the hands of a globally active company management. It is claimed that decentralization tends to shift the distribution of power in favor of the corporate central office, which can use new IT-based and target-oriented control mechanisms to exert pressure on the decentralized units. With these strategies there is no longer any need to control specific individuals or processes. It is sufficient to exerting control over whether targets are met.

A second line of discussion is informed by the theory of power and assumes that decentralization measures allow the leadership of an enterprise to gain greater influence because they enable managers to play one autonomous unit against the other. As a rule, independently operating profit centers have control over the important functional areas of production, purchasing, sales, quality assurance, construction, and personnel. Thus, they can be carved out of the overall organization without creating overwhelming complexity. This puts the corporation's central office in a position to set the profit centers in competition to one another and divest them if they perform poorly. And since the performance evaluation criteria are defined largely by the central office itself, it also has a considerable say with respect to the decentralization of entrepreneurial competencies.

A third line of argumentation can be found in governance theory and is based on the possibility that the different units of an organization can be coupled to or de-coupled from one another to different degrees. For example, Henry Mintzberg (Mintzberg 1979, 385f.) argues that the introduction of profit center structures represents only a partial decentralization of a holding company. Whereas relationships between divisions can indeed be loose, relationships within the individual divisions must be all the stronger because of their clear goal orientation. The introduction of divisionalization often has the effect that the individual independent units develop greater internal centralization and formalization than they had as non-autonomous organizations. This then leads to greater cohesion in the holding company.

The variations in nuance and in the underlying theories notwithstanding, all three lines of argumentation have in common the assumption that management deliberately links decentralization and centralization. It becomes clear that the emergence of the decentralization/centralization paradox is primarily considered the outcome of a strategic management decision. Paradoxical formulations such as "controlled autonomy," "externally managed self-organization," or "centralized decentralization" already speak to the hypothesis that a specific combination of decentralization and centralization is the result of a management strategy.

The value of research on the relationship of centralization and decentralization is that it differentiates the simplifying assumption of a wave-like alternation between these organizational strategies. It contrasts the frequently undifferentiated self-descriptions of reorganization projects as measures to promote "empowerment," "self-organization," and "intrapreneurship" with a more differentiated definition of the simultaneous occurrence of centralizing and decentralizing factors.

The Paradoxical Effects, Ancillary Consequences, and Dilemmas of Decentralization

The discussion of the polarity between decentralization and centralization can profit through greater openness to more recent approaches which address undesirable, paradoxical side effects and dilemmas in organizations. For example, Nils Brunsson (Brunsson 1989, 231f.) warned about assuming too close a connection between intentions and effects when analyzing organizations. While it is true that influential players propagate the idea that their strategies are logical and rational, it is not a foregone conclusion that these goals will also be achieved. According to Brunsson, the structures, processes, and ideologies that are observed do not necessarily correspond with those that the organization itself or a management theory would like to achieve.

Focusing on unplanned ancillary consequences, paradoxical effects, and costs that were not taken into account has made it possible to identify in the new forms of organization the main problem areas to which management's thinking on recentralization generally refer. Concepts such as "management overload," a "company policy dilemma," "sector egotism," an "identity dilemma," "Balkanization," the "participation paradox," a "politicization dilemma," and a "complexity explosion" indicate that greater differentiation into partially autonomous, self-organizing units makes overall integration in organizations become not only increasingly necessary, but also increasingly difficult.

Based on research conducted in organizations with leadership teams, it has now become possible to merge the discussion of simultaneous decentralization and centralization with that of undesirable ancillary consequences and paradoxical effects.

5.5 The Centralization of Decision-Making Competencies as an Undesired Side Effect of Decentralization

Contrary to the intentions of management, systematic decentralization produces the undesired side effect of a centralization of decision making. From this perspective, the resulting controlled autonomy, externally organized self-organization, or centralistic decentralization is an undesired outcome of the decentralization measures. The more strength Sisyphus exerts to roll the rock up the hill, the greater the momentum of the boulder as it crashes down again.

The new forms of business organization entail a specific, selective replacement of hierarchical management with coordination based on discursive agreement (see, among others, Sturdy/Wright/Wylie 2014). Whereas overall hierarchical management of the company is retained, the internal coordination of work units in the value-adding area is addressed primarily through discursive or consensual agreement. The goal is, as demonstrated above, to gain control over the undesired side effects of the hierarchy. Yet this does not need to result in a lessening of the hierarchy's importance, as already indicated by Farson (Farson 1997, 22).

Instead, the hierarchy is restructured in such a way that it defines, restricts, and imposes time limits on the use of group and team structures (see, for example, the informative work of Hodgson 2004, McSweeney 2006, and Hodgson/Briand 2013). When levels with group structures and levels with one-person leadership alternate, it can have the effect that the two levels mutually keep one another in check to the degree that the undesired side effects of the two respective forms of organization can be mitigated.

Nevertheless, when a number of levels with team and group structures are connected in series, it can happen—particularly in crisis situations—that the hierarchy's definition, restriction, and time limitation of group structures is not triggered until very late in the process. Then, in extreme cases, the structural problems of group work in the form of tedious decision-making processes, power struggles, and the diffusion of responsibility can proliferate for so long that they hit upon a hierarchical level with one-person leadership.

6.
Failure as Success
in Group Work Projects

"Changing the *formal* organization is sometimes the most effective way to influence the *informal* operating environment."
David A. Nadler

In the literature on management, industrial sociology, work science, and organizational psychology, in terms of new forms of organization, no other topic has been discussed as intensively and comprehensively as group work. This broad interest arose because group work is viewed as the central measure taken to turn away from Taylorism and embrace more holistic forms of work organization. Models such as "post-Fordism," the "new production concepts," and "operative decentralization" are based to a significant degree on the introduction of partially autonomous group work in the value-adding area of businesses.

In the meantime, the way group work functions has been described not only for key sectors such as the automotive, machine manufacturing, electronics, and chemical industries, but also for service businesses, government agencies, and hospitals. The case studies presented until now have concentrated primarily on the introduction of group work or on the way it functions shortly thereafter.

The major shortcoming of this research is that it consists almost exclusively of one-point studies. The status quo of work organization at a certain time is ascertained, and from that generalizable statements are derived. Longitudinal studies, multi-point studies, and re-evaluations of businesses are rare exceptions. On the one hand, this limitation is related to the short duration of the studies, while another explanation would be that researchers have committed themselves based on their previous publications. When researchers publish studies on group work, they commit themselves to statements which can later be refuted if the business is re-evaluated. As a result, the literature almost exclusively reports successes using group work; reports of failures or miscarried attempts with group work are virtually nonexistent in the business press and in scientific literature.

This chapter examines three businesses in which earlier researchers have conducted important consulting projects and studies on decentralization. In lectures and in print, these companies were (and in part still are) portrayed as organizations that pioneered decentralized structures. Yet while the public—which is primarily interested in the display side of organizations—has not registered it, two of the companies have in the interim altogether eliminated group work. The third is currently engaged in a process of recentralization and re-Taylorization.

In a midsized supplier to the automobile industry, which we will call Ladra, previously introduced customer and product-related production islands were dismantled and classical, process-oriented departments reintroduced. Indirect tasks such as personnel planning, order flow control, maintenance, and quality insurance which had initially been transferred to the competency of the islands, were once again consolidated into centralized departments. The group speakers were granted hierarchical authority. As the CEO put it, they once again "became a little bit like" department heads or shift leaders. According to the CEO, the entire business had now embarked on the road "back to the future."

In another company, which numbers among the world's leading machine manufacturing corporations, group work was allowed to tail off two years after it was introduced. In this company, which we will call Jamus, group work was based on weekly planning which was drawn up by the employees themselves in the production islands. Yet the job coordination office, which was intended to feed assignments to the groups, was already jettisoned after less than a year. The weekly planning schedules were worth no more than wastepaper and had no further effect on managing production. Rotation between jobs within the group, as practiced at the beginning of the group work endeavor, was halted. In the meantime, all of the employees once again have their set workplace. The offices of the group speakers have been abandoned. The little pool houses, where the groups' coordination efforts were to take place, have been torn down.

Practically speaking, all that is left to bear witness to group work is the positioning of the machinery and the signage over the group areas. At a midsized supplier to the automobile and machine building industry, which we will call Keymac, a process of recentralization is now underway following a very extensive decentralization. According to the observations of production and assembly workers, group work had dropped off in several areas. As a first step, there were indications that team-oriented leadership was being dismantled in favor of person-focused leadership. In a newly founded field office, it appeared that players who made a case for a classical Taylorist structure had gained the upper hand.

As a reaction to these findings, one might reflexively assume that businesses are in a recentralization trend. After every wave of decentralization, not only the business press, but also the fields of sociology and work science observe a trend toward re-Taylorization. For the automobile industry, which is often attributed a pioneering role in the implementation of new production concepts, the fact is then documented that attempts at partially autonomous group work have been rescinded in favor of more restrictive forms of work, and that forms of highly repetitive production line work with short cycle times become increasingly prevalent in the assembly areas.

Nevertheless, the debate over recentralization and re-Taylorization tendencies must not be limited to once again postulating a "return to old production concepts," a "Renaissance of the old rationalization types," "re- or neo-Fordism," or a "new narrow-mindedness" in the wake of "new types of rationalization," "post-Fordism," or "new broad mindedness." Rather, the findings pertaining to the rollback of group work should be used to expand the discussion of group work in the companies by selectively adding a perspective based on the theory of power, neo-institutionalism, or systems theory. A theoretical focus of this kind can complement the approaches of economics, work science, organizational psychology, and industrial sociology (and in part also challenge them to object). These approaches orient their interpretations of the new work forms primarily on criteria that supposedly can be objectively defined such as efficiency and productivity on one hand, and humanization of the workplace on the other.

In the first part (6.1) I discuss the question of why this form of work has been phased out once again in spite of the positive economic advantages seen in group work by management at the time and by the scientific researchers who facilitated it. Taking recourse to neo-institutionalist considerations, this section reconstructs that the efficiency or non-efficiency of group work is not an objectively definable parameter but rather a social construction of the respectively dominant coalition within the company. The second part (6.2) centers on the question of why employees offered hardly any resistance to the elimination of group work and in part actually welcomed it. By drawing on micro-political considerations about infractions of rules and on a differentiation between conditional and goal programs, I show that group work limited employees' ability to expand their sphere of influence; in part, they actually lost influence. Part three (6.3) explains why the concept of operative decentralization can be so easily eroded and why, once group work has been introduced, one finds hardly any structural inertia, no "lock ins," and no path dependency. Here, there is a tendency in group work for conditional programs to be replaced by goal programs. The personnel factor gains importance. Goal programs and human resources decision programming are, however, subject to far less structural inertia, and therefore facilitate the erosion of group work. In the concluding part (6.4), I discuss whether one is justified at all in speaking of a general failure of the group work concept in the three companies examined, or whether it is not instead a question of group work projects failing *successfully*.

6.1 The Relativity of the Efficiency Argument in Group Work

There is a large amount of research pointing out that group work accomplishes a wide range of optimizations: the shortening of through-put times, the reduction of unit costs and revolving stock, quality improvement, increased flexibility, decreased inventory, higher delivery quality, and scheduling reliability. In spite of all the discussion about which instruments can be used to measure its effectiveness, group work overall is considered positive in an economic sense. The results of meta-analyses show that group work has a positive effect on bottom line productivity. From this, one could conclude that self-regulating work groups are in a better position than a production system based on Taylorist principles to adapt to changing internal and external demands and that all in all this form of work leads to greater productivity.[8]

According to the logic of these scientific studies, the descriptions of the introduction of group work prepared by participating managers of the three companies, as well as the reports of the accompanying researchers, read as economic success stories. At Ladra, the effects of group work were described with catchwords such as "increased efficiency, lower overhead," "significant savings on overhead," "marked quality improvement and cost savings," and "improvement of international competitiveness through cost-effective organization." It was determined that revenue per hour worked increased by 50 percent in six years. At Jamus as well, the introduction of group work was judged as a success across the board. As an example, the positive development of revenue figures following the introduction of the new work form was viewed as a clear indication that desired effects such as a reduction of idle time and reworking had taken place. The production islands reduced production costs by up to 20 percent and decreased throughput time by up to 50 percent. At Keymac, too, it was also assumed that group work increased efficiency.

In light of these positive and in part euphoric assessments, the questions in this area are obvious. For all the positive ratings by management as well as the accompanying scientific researchers with respect to productivity, adherence to schedule, throughput time, and quality, why was group work revoked? Did the productivity calculations reflect the "objective" situation in the businesses or were they constructed to legitimize the measures taken?

---

8 Rather than citing a multitude of individual studies, I refer here only to the early meta-analysis conducted by Beekun (Beekun 1989).

The Relativity of the Efficiency Argument

The point of view that long dominated the discussion of group work is based on the premise that organizations have overarching goals (efficiency, humanization, etc.) which can be used to orient, evaluate, and sanction the behavior of employees. The rationality of the organization and therefore also the decision about potentially introducing group work are based on tough efficiency calculations. The implicit assumption is that the market situation and the overarching goals allow management to derive preferences and enable it to reach decisions between alternatives such as a Taylorist work form, restrictive group work, or partially autonomous value-adding islands. From this perspective, rationalizations are attempts to improve end-means relationships in organizations. According to this logic, to draw on a simile used by James March (March 1962, 669), organizations are like a tree that attempts to optimize its exposure to the sun; the growth of its leaves are subject to the tree's optimization strategy.

From an instrumental-rational perspective there are, broadly speaking, three approaches to explaining the elimination of group work. They already began to emerge in the 1970s as part of the discussion of the failed group work projects undertaken in various countries within the framework of programs to humanize the workplace. The first explanatory approach assumes that the framework conditions (the market, technology, logistics systems, the employee base, ownership structure, cross-company strategies, etc.) changed to such a degree that group work could no longer be seen as the most efficient form of work and was therefore abandoned. The second approach postulates a management learning process which, after phases of experimentation, measuring, and reflection, led to the insight that work forms other than partially autonomous group work offered greater advantages. The third explanation attempt is found frequently in group work literature and traces the problems that arise with group work, even though it is actually an economically superior concept, to avoidable factors such as "faulty design," "a halfhearted approach," employee ineptitude and ignorance, and egotistic interests. In that case, it is the reprehensible "micro-political interventions" that undermine a concept which is intrinsically successful and economically sensible.

Systems theoretical research challenges the instrumental-rational view of organizations at the fundamental level. These approaches do not express doubt that organizations have purposes. The doubt is directed at whether purposes and the means chosen to achieve them can be used to explain organizations. It is pointed out that organizations have a multitude of contradictory goals and that goal setting consequently cannot be used as a point of departure for organizational analyses. Organizations have numerous units with a wide range of preferences, inclinations, and goals. Decisions are the results of conflicts and/or compromises between the various units. Seen in those terms, and once again referencing James G. March's simile, organizations function like a tree where each individual leaf strives to catch the sunlight. Thus, the growth of the tree is merely the result of the conflicting interests of its leaves.

This theoretical approach opens up a new perspective on the discussion of efficiency, effectiveness, and profitability of group work. The limited rationality which serves as a basis for this theoretical concept also applies for profitability calculations that appear "hard" and "objective." Particularly in light of the notoriously "turbulent and uncertain environment," keeping framework conditions stable enough to allow an unequivocal attribution of effect to causes is possible only in exceptional cases. In a number of studies based on decision-making theory it has meanwhile been shown that there is a tendency in organizations to impute results even to situations that actually do not permit unequivocal quantification, and subsequently to assign monetary value to them. As well, tools for determining efficiency and effectiveness are often used in situations where their application can be judged inappropriate.

Efficiency and effectiveness, according to this line of thinking, can no longer be understood as a goal to which all actions refer. Instead, with respect to group work, efficiency-, effectiveness-, and profitability calculations are internally formed constructs the organization uses to connect with the management concepts circulating in the environment. Here, it is not so much a question of the veracity of the profitability calculations as the question of how the seemingly objective definition of efficiency and effectiveness "closes gaps," while at the same time "rendering the improbable probable." What matters is how and with what consequences the meaning generated by the calculations serves to orient and legitimize the actions of the players, and ultimately makes them appear necessary or unavoidable.

Early on, Ulrike Berger (Berger 1988, 127) pointed out that proof of efficiency and effectiveness lends a coalition's preferred alternative the appearance of being sound and economically rational, thereby increasing the chances that the preferred alternative will prevail. These calculations have the advantage that, compared to "softer" types of formal rationality, they use the hard "language of money." Even though the "translations" are very free, in businesses they have the advantage of being the "language of the land" because in capitalism the survival of a business depends on its financial solvency. Berger comes to the conclusion that from this point of view economic rationality does not appear so much a computable and unequivocally definable allocation principle, but as a myth which under conditions of uncertainty can be helpful in legitimizing actions and decisions internally as well as to the outside world.

The Construction of Efficiency and Effectiveness and the Argument over the Power to Interpret Them

Multi-point research on organizations enables us to bring to light the social construction of efficiency and effectiveness by various coalitions. At least two different coalitions with partially opposing interests occupied themselves with the profitability of group work in the companies examined. As a result, not only did significant discrepancies of evaluation arise, but the construction of the efficiency (or inefficiency) calculations of the different coalitions also came up for discussion.

In all three companies, Ladra, Jamus, and Keymac, economic crisis situations were the initial reason for the introduction of partially autonomous group work. In two of the cases, the holding company threatened to shut down, sell off, or relocate the subsidiary if management couldn't get out of the red ink. In the third company, a crisis in the automobile industry put management under pressure to strike out in new directions. Under these circumstances, the object was to open up some maneuvering room, especially for the two businesses operating under holding companies. At Ladra, it was particularly the board of directors that was pushing for new forms of production. After the company was acquired by a major overseas corporation, Ladra's board needed to prove to the new owner that it could gain control of its costs as well as its quality problems through new forms of work and production. At Jamus, management faced an ultimatum from the holding company: they could either get into the black within the next two years or the product line would be divested. The CEO initiated a change in the structure of the organization because referring to a sound, modern concept would not only enable him to obtain additional capital appropriations but also allow him to catch his breath.

From a neo-institutionalist perspective, it is not surprising that the companies oriented themselves on the current model of operative decentralization. Paul J. DiMaggio and Walter W. Powell (DiMaggio/ Powell 1983) cite the mechanism of mimetic isomorphy as one of the reasons for the striking homogeneity of organizational forms across the boundaries of corporations. Particularly under conditions of great uncertainty, for example, in economic crises, when organizations create structures they often draw on each other as models. They mimic the structures of organizations they either consider to be particularly successful, or those that play a central role in their environment, say, for their customers.

As an illustration, when automotive manufacturers—which pioneer the introduction of new production concepts in many cases—introduce group work, other smaller companies that supply them often quickly follow suit. Since automotive corporations represented the most important customer group for two of the three companies examined here, and the third business also kept a very watchful eye on developments in the automotive industry, group work played a central role in the decentralization strategies of the three companies. As the corporate development officer at Keymac reported, "We introduced group work because the other people were doing it.

It didn't matter what kind of catchphrases were on the market, our company participated." And a member of the sector team in the same company stated, "Midsized firms react to passing fashions … group work started at Mercedes, with sermons about group work. So then, naturally, as a direct supplier to Mercedes, the midsized firm has to introduce group work, too. They're not reacting out of conviction, they're reacting to trends."

Seminars, lectures, and conferences where current developments in key industries are reported play an important role in promulgating production concepts. Whereas the framework conditions of the holding companies played a central role for the two firms that were their subsidiaries, in the third, privately held company, much depended on the managing partner. "You have to think of it in very simple terms," the accompanying researcher at Keymac reported. "The business owner goes to conventions and hears presentations by professors who are saying that sector organization is important. So, then he says to the professor, aha, then why don't you introduce it at my firm … And then he (the professorial consultant) holds two or three events, and that costs a little money, and then he sends in his employees and they do a little of this and that, and then they say, 'OK, now you have sector organization.'"

Particularly in recent years, the neo-institutionalists have been discussing the danger that researchers base their assumptions on overly socialized behavior in organizations and have been neglecting intentional actions. Members of an organization then appear as nothing more than victims of socially legitimized expectations who are trapped in a "iron cage." The three firms under examination showed that reorganization processes in businesses do indeed orient themselves toward dominant models in their organizational environment, but that it required a coalition of company management and the personnel department, the employee representatives, and the accompanying external researchers to make reorganization possible within the framework of a dominant model. Even though all of the players espoused the rhetoric of buying into "saving the company," there were a large number of individual rationalities that led to the formation of coalitions.

As an example, the introduction of group work, and in particular the high visibility the company gained because of it, meant a significantly improved career outlook for executives. As the head of the employee organization at Ladra described it, just before the company's poor economic condition became known the director of human resources, highlighting his experience with group work, switched to a different company. The head of human resources for the entire concern, who had facilitated the introduction of the new forms of business organization, went into business for himself as a group work consultant and acquired his first assignments by pointing to his success at his previous company.

In all three businesses, management entered into a coalition with the employee organization which assumed a type of co-management role in the introduction of group work. The employee representatives at Jamus emphasized that they had been "strongly involved in the project" at the time and had become a "close partner" of company management. In fact, the employee organization had still continued to "push when company management had already begun to slack off. It was still our baby, too." At Ladra, the employee representative likewise sided with management and distanced himself from union headquarters which at the time was still taking a critical stance toward group work. "Our first works council agreement was a huge slash at the union line … And that's also why we threw the union out of here … We just started doing group work on our own … You can imagine how incredibly hard the unions came down on me for that." And at Keymac as well, "Close cooperation between management and the employee organization played an important role in the introduction of group work."

The third players in this coalition were the accompanying external researchers. In one case, the introduction of group work was facilitated by a semi-governmental research institute, which urgently needed the undertaking as a reference project. The institute used the group work project to advertise in its informational brochures on teambuilding, process analysis, and qualification guidelines, and invited managers from other businesses to participate. The CEO explained, "They carried the concept to the outside world so they could make other companies enthusiastic about it." The second group work project was accompanied by a work science research institute whose employees had made a name for themselves as group work experts. In the third business, a researcher in work science conducted a long-term study on group work.

From the perspective of current management in two of the three businesses examined, the dominant coalition of group work advocates used its strong hand at the time to determine in which groups, using which tools, and at which intervals profitability calculations would be undertaken, and how the data were to be interpreted. As a result, the evaluation of group work was artificially positive.

As a first piece of documentation, new management cited the fact that the profitability calculations were strongly based on experiences with pilot islands. All three companies experimented with pilot islands, and the supposedly positive experiences were used to justify further expansion of the group work models. From where the current CEO of one company stands, a deliberate decision was made to select a pilot island that would support the advantages of group work. Company management at the time chose an area that was "down and out." Subsequently, a group with the best people was set up to manufacture a product that was in relatively constant demand over the course of the entire year.

A second piece of evidence was that productivity gains were attributed to the introduction of group work, even though the attribution clearly had feet of clay. For example, in its external presentation one of the companies pointed out that the introduction of group work brought about visible productivity gains. Internally, meanwhile, the difficulty of defining productivity gains was being discussed. As the head of production at Keymac remarked, "I do not feel confident making a statement about how much of the productivity gains can be attributed to group work. I think we did achieve an increase, but it can't be measured." Thus, it was not possible to determine analytically the extent to which the construction of assembly lines (the reduction of buffers) and the introduction of group work respectively contributed to productivity gains.

The erosion of group work and an increasingly critical stance on the profitability of decentralized organizational structures were closely related to the collapse of the coalitions of those who advocated it. Particularly in businesses that worked with the automobile industry, it became apparent that group work in its partially autonomous form was no longer necessarily *en vogue*. For that reason, pressure to introduce partially autonomous groups also decreased on supplier companies. One of the master craftsmen at Keymac stated, "Now the coming trend … is that Mercedes, BMW, and Opel are moving away from it. And in the USA, entirely different things are going on. So, I'm convinced that it won't take long here either before we have disciplinary superiors in the group and in the sector team." An employee from the company's production department told us, "The development has already happened. BMW, Mercedes, Opel, they don't have self-governing groups anymore. The only way it works is with a manager. It'll happen faster than we think. In less than three years you won't find a single group anymore that doesn't have that manager, a direct superior. I'm totally sure of it."

Particularly in the two companies where we not only saw a silent erosion of group work but later also conscious strategic decisions to recentralize, the elimination of group work was justified through a lack of efficiency and profitability. The CEO of one firm explained, "You can kid yourself for a long time, but when you can document that productivity … is heading south, then you have to change things." And yet, paradoxically, the reasons the companies cited in support of recentralization were the very ones that had been used to justify the introduction of group work. In one firm, for example, it was pointed out that if incoming orders remained constant the customer-specific groups worked at capacity, and rationalization gains could be achieved. When incoming orders fluctuated, however, serious problems arose because the groups experienced phases of underutilization. In another company, it was argued that the employees involved in group work frequently developed specialization in one specific task. It was only the recentralized structure and the strengthening of the master craftsman level that put the first management echelon in a position to urge employees to work at different machines more often.

A Perspective: The Deconstruction of Efficiency Definitions

The assumption of the companies' new management that classical process-oriented work organization is more efficient than group work is likewise a social construction that is based on simplifications and attributions that can be problematized. Yet it is more difficult to demonstrate the way this assumption is constructed because it currently represents the dominant perspective. It is only the former promoters of group work in the businesses who question the efficiency measures new management is taking. They attempt to prove that the profitability calculations used to document the superiority of process-oriented production methods rest on dubious premises and serve only to legitimize centralistic reorganization projects.

The promoters as well as the opponents of group work systems are not entirely at liberty in the social construction of efficiency and effectiveness calculations. The principle of financial reproduction is a structural factor that cannot be arbitrarily deceived. Nevertheless—and this is the central difference in the approaches of the advocates compared to the opponents of group work—the profitability principle is not the "autonomous primal source" from which alone all economic and strategic action must be derived. Efficiency, effectiveness, and profitability are initially no more than empty phrases that need to be filled with content and brought to life by the players who allegedly derive their actions from them.

6.2 The Humanization Argument with a Dash of Power Theory: Group Work as an Employee Barter Exchange

The dominant group work thread in the literature emphasizes that group work not only provides efficiency advantages for organizations but additionally achieves greater employee satisfaction with their jobs. Studies conducted in the framework of the Scandinavian "Quality of Worklife" program (Lattmann 1972, 54) established early on that group work increased productivity, but that employees also found their activities more interesting and richer in variety than the jobs they previously performed by themselves. Later research as well was based on the overall assumption that moderate to highly autonomous group work had a beneficial effect over the mid to long term on motivation, the employees' attitude toward the business, and social and cognitive attendance (Weber 1997, 41ff.). Thus, the majority of scientific studies support the argumentation that is well-established in management literature and in practice, namely, that the new work structures bring about win-win situations that connect productivity improvement with humane job design. It is said that company leaders profit from greater efficiency and employee motivation, while employees are assigned interesting tasks and have an opportunity to participate directly in structuring their work environment.

There are only isolated reports of employee resistance to the introduction of group work. Such resistance is generally explained merely as employees' "defensive routines." Particularly employees who previously performed narrowly defined tasks are said to doubt whether their qualifications are adequate for the holistic approach in group work and resist taking on new activities. The literature, which is often normatively charged, points out that the problems with defensive employees are not structural in nature and can be remedied by informing employees at an early stage, including them in the design process, by qualifying those who are not team material, and creating corresponding positions for them. Resistance, conflict, confrontations and in some cases stagnation are said to be normal during the introduction phase, but as the process unfolds they supposedly subside in light of the benefits group work provides for employees.

In the companies examined, the advocates of group work assessed this form of work organization as beneficial and meaningful for employees. At Ladra, for example, it was said that the humanization of the work environment was an additional goal of everyone involved. As the company's former employee spokesperson put it, "The fact that employees could become involved was initially a positive thing for everybody." In two of the businesses, this assessment was largely shared by the accompanying scientific researchers as well.

The hope that group work would lead to a humanization of the workplace and strengthen the position of employees was also a reason why the unions, after some initial skepticism, particularly at Jamus and Keymac, supported the initiatives. As an example, while visiting one of the companies a board member of a major regional labor union announced that "the philosophy behind order-driven production islands and the associated concept of production planning and control are very interesting." They represented, he stated, "a very positive example" and a "step toward the humanization of the workplace" and had a "certain role model character." The union leader concluded with, "We will be making the pilgrimage here frequently in the future."

Given the positive assessment of the humanization effects by management, the accompanying researchers, and the labor unions, it is surprising that the employees did not block or prevent the rollback of group work in a company which, according to the CEO, had actually responded "very positively." The lack of resistance is surprising because industrial sociology, with its interest in political constellations of action, points out how difficult it is to dismantle institutionalized influence and power structures. The argument is that the established power structures have the tendency to resist change because any reorganization could throw the unstable balance of power in a company into confusion.

An examination of the humanization argument involves a series of power theory-oriented research questions. Why is it that employees do not resist the revocation of group work, even though the literature alleges that this form of work organization allows them to gain influence? Which new zones of uncertainty do employees control in partially autonomous group work; which do they lose compared to a classical Taylorist structure? How does the transition from tasks based on detailed instructions to leadership through target agreements influence the distribution of power?

The Hybrid Character of Power,
and Skepticism about Group Work

Employees who can assert their will over others command a central source of power based on their control of zones of uncertainty with respect to competencies, contacts in the environment, or authority. There is no doubt that an employee with hierarchical authority, who enjoys a privileged relationship with important customers, and additionally numbers among the few people who control a complicated production planning system, has good chances of asserting her interests.

Another, often overlooked source of power lies in the discrepancy between players' actual opportunities for action and the officially formulated actions required of them. In micro-political games, opportunities to act become particularly valuable when the actions cannot be enforced through directives, regulations, or job descriptions, but are instead performed as "voluntary," informal barters that must be repaid at a later time.

This point is key in terms of the lack of employee resistance against the elimination of group work. Organizational theory assumed that the success of organizations in modern society is based on the existence of an elaborate set of regulations that coordinate and control organizational processes, and that the members of organizations also abide by them. Meanwhile, empirical research beginning as early as the middle of the 20th century has shown that there is a large discrepancy between the blueprints of an organization and the way operations unfold in reality. It was ascertained that the goal of an organization cannot be to reduce deviations from formal structures to the greatest degree possible. On the contrary, the way an organization functions depends significantly on the acceptance of deviations from formal structures. Working by the book would cause any organization to break down. It would collapse under its own rigidity.

This is where we encounter the "paradox of the organigram." Official structures and formal regulations cause problems because they cannot be adapted to all the demands of day-to-day operations and therefore cannot (or are not permitted to) prevent deviations. Rules that are actually intended to reduce uncertainty in an organization necessitate daily infractions which, in turn, introduce new uncertainty. Although regulations supply fixed points that can be used to orient decisions, this is counteracted by the fact that deviations from these rules must always be taken into consideration as well. In practice, an organization's rules must be applied in a way that adapts them to respective situations but also permits deviation from the rules without rendering them completely inoperative.

There are good reasons why such functional deviations relating to the entire organization cannot be programmed in the form of "explicit deviation instructions." Frequently, the exceptions cannot be defined in advance with such precision that they can be adapted to the sequence of events in the form of rules. In part, instructions for deviation that are too explicit would be detrimental to the earnestness of the basic regulations. For that reason, tacit acceptance of deviations is preferable. Also, in some instances formulating deviation rules would require mobilizing a large number of quarreling organizational entities, making it appear unlikely that a deviation rule would be formulated officially (Luhmann 2000, 265).

A willingness to deviate from rules when "it is in the interest of the organization" has always been implicitly required of employees. Nevertheless, it cannot—and herein lies the peculiarity—be enforced through the formal sanctioning options of the hierarchy. And it is this very discrepancy between officially stipulated obligations and actually expected job requirements that can serve as a source of power and influence, even for employees at low levels of the hierarchy. Important resources are created which are traded on the organization's barter exchanges. The possibility (and necessity) of controlling the performance of one's job independently and the functional redefinition of duties, as already indicated in the 1960s by David Mechanic (Mechanic 1962), provide de facto opportunities to exert influence for employees who are supposedly powerless.

The Threat of Employees Losing Power through the Transition from Conditional to Goal Grogramming

My proposition is that a partial rearrangement in the programs curtails the sphere of influence of employees in the organization's value-adding core. Organizations use programs to create criteria that can be used to make statements about the correctness of decisions. Decision-making programs presuppose that compliance or lack of compliance with them can always be discerned. Yet that does not mean they have to be defined in detail. Demanding that someone "See to it that the unit ultimately generates at least a 10 percent return on sales" can be understood, the lack of precision notwithstanding, as an action guiding decision-making program.

James G. March and Herbert Simon (March/Simon 1958, 164ff.) differentiate between two types of programs: conditional programs and goal programs. *Conditional programs* are "if-then programs" that prescribe certain ways in which the members of an organization must behave in response to a previously defined stimulus. If the stimulus occurs, it is expected that a stipulated sequence of actions will be set in motion. As an example, in assembly line production the receipt of a previously specified part is the stimulus for the initiation of formalized and codified sequences of action. Conditional programs do not require that players seek solutions of their own. Such programs create a high degree of predictability (or at least an illusion thereof) because they are designed for repetition over the long term and can produce consistent decision-making behavior when similar stimuli occur (Luhmann 1969, 130).

Goal programs, in contrast, are geared to desired effects. They merely specify goals. Members of the organization are expected, while taking secondary conditions into consideration, to find the appropriate means to accomplish their goals. Goal programs require only that a certain amount of work be accomplished; it is left up to the employees themselves which means they use to accomplish the assignment. Compared to conditional programs, goal programs are more future oriented because they do not determine in advance which means must be used to react to a given impulse (Luhmann 2000, 256ff.).

Organizations always resort to both kinds of programs, but the program types are also combined with one another in different ways depending on environmental conditions, management strategies, or work organization. When group work is introduced, a selective transition from conditional programs to goal programs takes place in the coordination of work in the value-adding core. Putting it in the language of the practitioners, the shift could be aptly summed up as, "They don't tell us how to do our jobs anymore; they just say what kind of results they want." Yet the only thing that matters, as they say, is the bottom line.

The transition from conditional to goal programming is most obvious in management by objectives. When the changeover to group work took place in the three companies discussed, employees were no longer required to follow strict routines, but only to meet the goals that had been set at the beginning of the week, month, or year. As an example, in one company at the beginning of every week a pool of orders was determined in a consultation between the order planning department and the group. Over the following days, the group had to work through the orders. Internal coordination, the choice of technical means, and the amount of time required to accomplish the goal, within the framework of the work assigned, were left to the discretion of the group. Goal programming has an effect on quality management as well. With conditional programming, the potential for optimization is achieved to a large degree through the company improvement system, and the often technically based routines and regulations are changed accordingly. When the transition to goal programming takes place, the centrally directed optimization measures apply only to the interfaces between the groups. In contrast, the improvement of internal group work processes—in other words, the optimization of the means—is left up to the groups and is no longer necessarily standardized and formalized. This means that in the framework of continuous improvement processes groups are literally expected to deviate from the rules, and the deviations are no longer even registered by their superiors.

But how does the distribution of power in the organization change through the transition from conditional to goal programs? One's first impression might be that the influence of the employees in groups and assembly islands increases. They take over zones of uncertainty that were previously controlled by master craftsmen or the operation planning, order planning, quality assurance, and construction departments. In the companies examined, however, the members of the groups adopted a somewhat ambivalent attitude in this question. At Ladra, it was noted that the tasks of the groups were not expanded to such a degree that the employees would have been able to assume a position of greater power. At Jamus, where specialized production workers wielded influence even under the traditional conditions due to the complexity of their jobs, simplified processes were indeed observed in the very beginning but an overall expansion of the groups' sphere of influence was not reported. At Keymac, particularly the groups in mechanical production with experienced technicians balked at group work because they saw no advantage for themselves.

The reason for this skepticism toward group work is that employees' opportunities for action are more pronounced with conditional programs than would appear at first glance. It is correct that conditional programs provide a good defense for management against employees refusing to cooperate because refusal is immediately obvious. Yet conditional programs also offer protection for employees because they represent secure roles for the people involved. The very fact that with conditional programs everything that is not permitted is forbidden makes it possible for employees to evade what is required of them. Everyone knows what to expect and what they are permitted and not permitted to do. This offers protection from the whims of the powerful in the organization because employees can always fall back on following the rules correctly and are absolved of unlimited responsibility and risky decisions.

Employees were able to selectively play deviations from these programs and the associated forfeiture of such protection as a trump card when trading on internal power exchanges. Thus, the highly elaborate rules, detailed instructions, bureaucratic regulations, and precisely specified working hours represented more than just restrictions for employees; in addition, they always served as negotiating points with superiors when deviations from the rules became necessary. In my opinion, the explanation for the lack of employee interest in group work, or their interest in seeing it rolled back, is that at the bottom line the introduction of group work did not increase employees' actual influence. Granted, employees were given greater control over customer contacts, but the introduction of new work-time models and target orientation caused them to lose negotiating power with management. Lost as bargaining chips in negotiations with company leadership, was the possibility and willingness of employees to stay on the job beyond the defined core time or to deviate from stipulated work processes. It also became impossible to receive compensation in the form of perks in other areas for pointing out errors in the program. Likewise, shirking responsibility was no longer possible in the same form, because there were now globally set targets.

Applying this to a famous example from the tobacco industry that was presented by sociologists Michel Crozier and Erhard Friedberg (Crozier/ Friedberg 1977), the sole reason the maintenance workers were so powerful was because they were (or had to be) managed through conditional and not goal programs. The maintenance workers received instructions that if the stimulus "a machine stops working" occurs, then they were to initiate the necessary courses of action. The game the maintenance workers played consisted of allowing so many problems to arise in the machines that maintenance was perceived as a crucial source of uncertainty in the company, while the maintenance workers themselves could not be accused of unprofessionalism. If programming at this point had been changed from conditional to goal programming—for example, an annual rate of 98 percent machine availability—the maintenance workers would have gained greater authority in organizing their work, but they would no longer have been able to control the zones of uncertainty in the same form.

An examination of the hybrid character of power could provide an explanation for why the introduction of group work is frequently viewed with skepticism, particularly by technicians in the production area. The difficulty of standardizing production tasks and the technicians' skill in dealing with them gives technicians in Taylorist work structures a considerable amount of informal influence. Studies of production units in machine construction companies that are organized along Taylorist lines were able to demonstrate that technicians gain influence by declaring themselves willing to take a flexible approach to rigid instructions in order to guarantee the on-time delivery of machinery—even though their instructions would not oblige them to adopt a goal program orientation. Yet when group work is introduced, goal programs obligate them to be flexible, subject to order flow, and to complete products on schedule. They face the threat of losing the informal flexibility bonus they previously enjoyed.

To sharpen the argument: the main thrust of group work research proceeds from the assumption (and with good reason) that employee resistance becomes particularly virulent in businesses where the form of group work introduced is restrictive, structurally conservative, or implemented in a halfhearted way. Yet based on the perspective developed in this chapter, we can conclude that, especially in the partially autonomous, structurally innovative, and enthusiastically implemented version of group work, a goal programming-based target agreement system causes employees to forfeit their previous ability to play the trump card of "informal flexibility." Therefore, in terms of power, group work only appears to be attractive for players in production and assembly units when it expands their formal options for action but does not overly erode the informal power potential they gain through their willingness to functionally deviate from the rules. When there is a changeover from conditional to goal programming, however, this is obviously the exception rather than the rule.

6.3 The Missing Lock-In: The Erosion of Group Work

One of the central questions is why Taylorist production methods based on the division of labor are capable of such persistence, and why it is so difficult for partially autonomous group work to establish itself as an alternative rationalization concept. In general, it is pointed out that the current rationalization strategies run up against rationality patterns in the form of tried-and-true techniques and ingrained routines that have evolved over many years. The past has shown these Taylorist rationality patterns to be reliable, and they therefore prove resistant to changes undertaken in the direction of more holistic forms of work.

This line of thinking is similar to the approaches in organizational theory that occupy themselves with the question of why organizations are so resistant to attempts to change them. Expressions such as "organizational inertia" (Hannan/Freeman 1977), "defensive routines" (Argyris 1985), "functional conservatism" (Child/Ganter/Kieser 1987), "deadlocks" (Brunsson 1989), "lock-ins" (Grabher 1993), and "path dependence" (David 1986) are used to point out that current decisions are always based on decisions made in the past, thereby restricting the opportunities to act.

The negative connotation of concepts such as inertia, lock-ins, or defensive routines notwithstanding, these approaches toy with a central ambivalence of organizations. The definition of rules and procedures is necessary because it is only through this that consistent perception and action become possible. Yet there is always the danger that the members of the organization content themselves with such definitions. The basic idea is that for employees, routine patterns of action relieve the pressure of undertaking constant reinterpretations. In that sense, they are functional for the organization. But they also cause organizations to become snared in proven patterns of behavior and therefore unreceptive to changes in the environment.

An approach that seems obvious but yields at best limited new insight would be to explain complaints over the persistence of Taylorist production methods through organization theoretical considerations on structural inertia, lock-ins, or path dependency. This leads to the conclusion that the path of Taylorist production methods based on the division of labor has been drawn so narrowly that new approaches can only establish themselves with difficulty, if at all.

This dominant perspective treats the topic of group work as if it had never fully established itself, and its promoters were still laboriously working their way through the established paths and defensive routines of the old form of organization. It is pointed out that group work was never introduced in the entire company, that the framework conditions such as remuneration for working hours were not adjusted, and as a result only "islands of group work" formed that were threatened by existing "classical" forms of work. Group work problems are then primarily cast as problems encountered with its introduction and not as the structural difficulties of a decentralized form of organization.

In this chapter, I would like to rephrase the question: why is it that production methods based on partially autonomous group work have such difficulty establishing themselves as a dominant path and, in contrast to Taylorist production methods, do not present themselves as lock-ins? What explains the relapses into Taylorist forms of work even though, according to the concept of decision-making corridors, in reforms there is (almost) no way back.

Reversing the direction of the questions seems sensible for two reasons. First, it allows us to trace the difficulties of establishing group work to structural characteristics of this production concept and not have to explain it exclusively through a lack of commitment on the part of company management, resistance at the middle management level, or technical errors. Second, it allows us to add to the discussion of structural inertia, lock-ins, and path dependency the question of why certain forms of organization do not present themselves (or only to a very limited degree) as defining a decision-making corridor.

Conditional Programs, Technization, and Lock-Ins

The concepts of lock-ins and path dependency stem from American technology research and were subsequently generalized for application to organizational phenomena. The basic idea of a lock-in and path dependency is that it is not respectively the most efficient organizational solution that prevails, but that current decisions are bound to a corridor or path by decisions that were made previously. The QWERTY keyboard design, to draw on a hackneyed example of a lock-in, represented the most sensible arrangement of the letters at the time it was introduced in the middle of the 19th century because this suboptimal arrangement of the keys alone was able to decrease the speed of typists and thereby prevent the type bars from jamming. Today, with computers and optimized typewriters, sticking type bars no longer pose a problem, but although an ergonomically more efficient keyboard arrangement would be appropriate, no change is taking place because the investment in learning to use a new keyboard would be too great (David 1985).

The central question is one that organizational sociology has left aside until now: to what extent can this description, which is so plausible for technical processes, be generalized to include processes in organizations overall? The inner structure of a technical machine involves an extreme form of conditional programming. Causes and effects are determined simultaneously. Because of the tight linkage between cause and effect, processes occur quasi automatically and are no longer interrupted by decisions. In a technical process an input is differentiated solely according to its condition of absolute identity or absolute difference, and in accordance with that a previously defined process is either set in motion or not. Social systems, too, as Luhmann (Luhmann 2000, 263/370) importantly added, can function very similarly to such technical machines, as long as the individuals involved are asked only to perform routine tasks and not to make decisions.

Technologies lead to strong path dependency because conditional programming relies on precise elaboration of if-then definitions, and such relationships are difficult to unwind. Technologies are characterized by interdependencies that depend on a frictionless meshing of the individual elements. If parts of a conditional program are changed, then, because of the tight connections, the other elements are automatically affected as well. Since interventions into the way an organization functions entail highly critical calculations that are extremely difficult to make, when systems based on conditional programming are involved, one often encounters the maximum, "Never touch a running system."

There is a structurally built-in mechanism in conditional programs that leads to self-stabilization of the program structure. For example, the use of a technology—due to the associated investment in production planning systems, machines, and personnel training—increases the probability that this technology will continue to be pursued. The investments in production planning systems, machines, and training the personnel who will be brought into line with the conditional programs represent "sunk costs" that limit the possibilities for change in an organization (Hannan/Freeman 1977, 931f.).

Turning away from Taylorist production concepts is difficult because it is a type of organization that is strongly based on conditional programs that manifest as formalized work processes, technologies (assembly-line production), production planning systems that are programmed in detail, and job descriptions. The great significance of conditional programs for Taylorist concepts makes this form of organization difficult to change because the "sunk costs" entailed are very high.

As portrayed in the previous section, introducing group work causes an easing of conditional programs as well as a partial transition to goal programs, and this shift appears to have an effect on the stability of group work.

The Decision-Making Premise Model and the Increased Importance of Personnel in Group Work

What structural changes take place in an organization when group work is introduced, and how do these structural changes relate to the ease with which group work can be eroded?

First suggested by Herbert A. Simon and later developed by Niklas Luhmann, the model of decision-making premises puts us in a position to analyze organizational structures without slipping into the static understanding of organizations seen in structural functionalism. According to Luhmann's basic thinking, decision-making premises guarantee that decisions in an organization reference one another in the first place and thereby ensure the organization's ability to reproduce. The three types of premises, namely, conditional and goal programs (for example, assembly-line production or management by objectives), the organization of competencies and communication channels (for example, hierarchies), and personnel (for example, hiring lawyers exclusively) limit the space of contingency of decisions that can be expected. A production line increases the probability that an automobile will be assembled on a conveyor belt and the body panels will not be randomly shuffled across the factory floor. Hierarchies and co-signing authority define competencies and communication channels and prevent everyone from making (or having to make) decisions on every matter. Hiring lawyers increases the likelihood that problems will be resolved in court rather than through mutual agreement.

Luhmann (Luhmann 2000, 222ff.) pointed out that the three types of decision-making premises represent functional equivalents and thereby create a basis for a change-oriented understanding of structures. The three kinds of decision-making premises are mutually interchangeable. If an organization places less value on qualified personnel, then it is to be expected that there will be an increase in the demands placed on the quality of the decision-making programs and the organization of communication channels. If hierarchies are flattened, pressure increases for personnel to be better qualified or for the programs to be more accurately designed.

The introduction of group work as an organizational concept represents a particular challenge because a reduction of conditional programming and the number of hierarchical levels goes hand-in-hand with a reduction in importance of two proven types of premises, namely, conditional programs and the organization of communication channels and competencies in the form of hierarchies. As a result, the decision-making premise of personnel gains importance. Research on public administrations has already ascertained that when rigid conditional programs are canceled and there is a shift of emphasis to relatively open goal programs, the personal characteristics, professional orientations, and decision-making styles of executives have a stronger effect (Koch 1993). In the companies described above, a parallel development could be observed. After the introduction of group work, the players involved emphasized the increased importance of personnel. In the company where elements of group work could still be observed, a particular increase in the importance of the personnel premise type was recorded: an employee survey conducted by the personnel department drew particular attention to the increased importance of the personnel factor after the introduction of group work.

The Problems with the Personnel Decision-Making Premise

In my view, the central importance of the personnel decision-making premise is the reason that group work can slowly (and sometimes in the absence of a formal decision) erode to the point where this form of organization is rescinded. At Jamus, a leading advocate of group work emphasized that initially there was no formal decision pertaining to the cancellation of group work. According to the company's former employee representative, "It happened very quietly, it was just rolled back a little bit." At Ladra, likewise, there was no formal decision on canceling group work; the rehierarchization was subtle. The group speakers, who had assumed a strong position in the company as coordinators and had also received privileges and financial perks, had, in the words of the CEO, "gradually morphed into master craftsman." And at Keymac as well, it was observed that group work was silently allowed to lapse. In some production and assembly units, the groups no longer elected speakers, group discussions no longer took place, and a strategy of successfully "muddling through" was adopted.

How are the personnel factor and the erosion of group work related? The sociological discussion of organizational learning and knowledge management has implicitly drawn attention to the weakness of this decision premise. It has been pointed out that while learning in individuals, particularly among top executives, represents an important resource for an organization, it is even more important to create an organizational memory for what has been learned. The problem with individual learning is that it is difficult to translate experience into business routines, and when individuals leave the organization, the knowledge is lost (Hedberg 1981).

The "personnel paradox" consists of this: individuals themselves are difficult to change, and forms of organization that rest heavily on the personnel decision premise are very unstable. Due to the circular interaction of internal and external perception of the self, it is difficult to change a specific member of a company, if the person can be changed at all. Many personnel development measures fizzle because employees resist being changed as individuals. If suitable staffing has resulted in a functioning team, changing its composition can cause big problems because programs and hierarchies can ensure cooperative relationships only to a limited degree.

In the businesses examined, the people surveyed pointed to the fragility and instability of this decision-making premise. An initial observation in the companies was that group work depended on a broad-based willingness of employees at the various levels to participate in this production concept. Group work quickly faces the danger of eroding when individual players exercise restraint with respect to the concept. At Jamus, for example, reluctance on the part of employees in the job controlling department as well as the master craftsman contributed significantly to the erosion of the concept. A former group speaker reported, "Group work was flatly undermined when there was a rush job, and the executives attached the well-known 'top priority,' 'extremely urgent,' or 'rush' labels to the components. That made it difficult for the groups to manage by themselves." At Keymac, group work could no longer be enforced in certain areas after experienced technicians in particular pointed out that it was all useless and were no longer willing to participate in group discussions. As the quality manager described it, "For many employees, not working in a group is simple. They come to work in the morning, and they know, 'This is my job, this is what I do' … and then they try to do it as simply as they can, (and) keep their responsibility to a minimum … As long as there are a certain number of employees who think like that, and it's not turned into some other mechanism from the outside … they're the ones who will prevail."

A second observation was that the group work system is extremely vulnerable when staffing fluctuates. At Ladra and Jamus, the critical economic situation led to terminations. As a result, some of the existing groups were torn apart. A laboriously created balance was upset, and in several groups the employees had little inclination to resume their coordination tasks. At Keymac, the situation was reversed. An economic boom urgently necessitated the hiring of new employees, but the existing staff saw this as a problem for working in groups. The rapid integration of new employees, floaters, and temporary staff created tension in some of the groups and brought about an internal resignation in some of the established employees.

The third observation was that maintaining group work requires ongoing investment in the personnel factor. In the opinion of those who promote decentralized business structures, maintaining group work requires continuous investment of resources. The corporate development officer at Keymac told us, "We were too quick to sit back and say that group work functions here … You can't think, well, I've introduced group work, and now it's up and running." The tenor in all three businesses was that group work functions only if executives, corporate development, and the consultants are constantly involved in personnel development.

Several employees commented on the problem of the strong focus on the personnel premise type by pointing to "human imperfections." An employee representative remarked, "Yes, it's great, but you can't put it into practice the way it's described on paper. Doesn't work … just too many human factors." One of the people we interviewed sarcastically expressed the hope that there would be scientific progress in the field of human genetics: "Group work might function—if gene research makes some progress."

Group Work's Split Lock-In

In group work, a split lock-in can be observed. On the one hand, it appears to establish itself as an organizational concept in such a way that it is difficult for management not to officially endorse group and teamwork in some form. In contrast to other models, such as lean management, business process reengineering, kaizen, or total quality management, the concept of group work does not appear subject to the half-life times usually seen in management discussions. On the other hand, in organizational practice no sufficiently compelling path develops that would be difficult for organizations to abandon. The decision-making corridor created by the introduction of group work seems to have very weak boundaries. This split lock-in aggravates the often-observed discrepancy between an organization's external presentation and its operational reality as perceived internally by employees.

6.4 The Successful Failure
of Group Work Projects

An obvious reaction to all this would be to view at least two of the three group work projects studied as failures. At Ladra and Jamus, the groups have practically no autonomy anymore with respect to job controlling, order planning, maintenance, logistics, quality assurance, and personnel planning. In some cases, they have been completely dismantled. For many employees, particularly in production, the introduction of group work is an episode they would rather forget. Nevertheless, this interpretation would mean viewing group work projects from an instrumental-rational perspective, which we have called into question above. One would be viewing group work under the criterion of a promising means to increase business efficiency and effectiveness, and group work's inability to establish itself as a failure of that means.

Rather than designating the group work projects as failures out of hand, we would like to cast them as reorganization measures that have "failed successfully." Research on inefficient and ineffective organizations that were able to survive in niches of the welfare state has elaborated that their success relates to their ability to internally model the contradictory demands of the environment and mobilize the support of important interest groups (Meyer/Zucker 1989). These insights into the functioning of organizations that are failing successfully can be transferred to businesses in the market economy. I would briefly like to point out two effects.

First, in at least two of the companies group work in any event gave management important room to maneuver. By associating with the decentralized production concepts that were gaining traction at the time, the CEOs once again managed to convince the holding companies to make substantial investments in their loss-making businesses. These funds were subsequently used for reorganizing the form of production, but also for the acquisition of new machinery. In the framework of the group work project, according to an employee in one of the companies, "They bought machines like they were a dime a dozen." By pointing out that the emerging efficiency increases could be attributed to group work, the companies were able to weather a difficult phase. When the economic situation began to improve, the board of the holding company was only marginally interested in whether the improved results could actually be traced to the new production concepts or (more likely) to changed market conditions.

Second, it was observed that the introduction of group work, particularly in the firms working with the automobile industry, represented an additional selling point that improved sales opportunities in their core market. According to the former employee representative of one company, "Group work was certainly a good form of external advertising." And the former employee representative of another company told us, "Frankly, you'd have to admit that because everyone was talking about Jamus, that was the reason for one customer or the other, maybe indirectly or subconsciously, staying with us, or maybe someone else became a new customer."

By pointing to these aspects of successfully failed group work projects, it is not our intention to introduce a more encompassing concept of instrumental rationality through the back door. It is a banal insight that preserving solvency is a central survival criterion for organizations in general and businesses in particular. However—and this is an important addition—remaining solvent is one criterion among others, and not the sole criterion to which organizations gear all of their activities, or according to which they are to be evaluated. Striving for profit represents a constraint, a necessary condition, and not an objective, which is to say, an overarching goal. Even though striving for financial reproduction plays a key role in a business's discussions, there is always a continually changing mix of purposes, targets, values, and interests.

This differentiation also allows us to observe the introduction and elimination of group work under entirely different aspects than merely increasing efficiency or inefficiency. It opens the perspective that even though, in the eyes of some executives and employees, the hoped-for immediate gains in efficiency and effectiveness did not materialize, these reorganization projects—albeit planned and intentional only to a limited degree—did make a contribution to the companies' survival. Not only the granting of a reprieve, but also the approval of additional funding and the effect of the new form of organization as a further selling point were to a large extent undesired ancillary effects that contributed to the businesses' survival.

7.
Innovation in Spite of Imitation

"Most imitators attempt the inimitable."
Marie von Ebner-Eschenbach

There are obvious reasons for a manager to fall into line with the respective dominant models of "successful organizations," "good management," and "efficient organizational leadership." The models free managers from the need to justify themselves and minimize their risk of being held accountable for a wrong decision. For example, during a time when decentralized organizational structures are *en vogue*, managers who choose a pronounced Taylorist form of production that is based on the division of labor will need to justify themselves, even if their businesses are economically successful.

Due to the complexity of the decision-making situation, it is often difficult to make decisions about efficient value-adding processes. Decision-makers often do not weigh more than a small number of alternatives against one another and do not make an attempt to think through in detail every variation of the decision, orienting themselves instead on ideas of suitability (March 1994, 100ff.). Rather than engaging in laborious discussions and decision-making processes and designing new approaches that require justification, they orient themselves on what is viewed by those in their environment as an appropriate way of proceeding, for example, by their customers, competitors, suppliers, researchers, political entities, and the media. There are many regulations, positions, procedural instructions, and programs that exist solely because they are seen by the environment as successful, rational, and modern. Whether they actually lead to more efficient internal procedures is a question that the decision-making process often does not examine.

Paul J. DiMaggio and Walter W. Powell (DiMaggio/Powell 1983) labeled this tendency to adapt to environmental expectations as "isomorphy," thereby describing the process that causes an organization to resemble other organizations that are active in the same or similar fields. From their perspective, the mechanism that is particularly prominent, aside from conforming due to (legal) constraints and normative pressure, is imitation. Uncertainty as to what the right approach could be causes organizations to respond with mimesis. They copy other organizations considered to be especially successful.

This allows organizational scientists to offer a good explanation of why organizations in the same field have a strong resemblance. European businesses orient themselves on the model of their US competitors whom they believe to be particularly successful. Large expert consulting firms define the way an efficient organization should look and cause their clients to adopt the model. Businesses undergoing reorganization processes that are fraught with uncertainty orient themselves on their competitors who are considered best-practice companies.

Although the category of isomorphy does a good job at describing the diffusion of ideas about "sound management," it is nevertheless difficult to use it as an explanation for innovations, transition, and changes in organizational models. To the degree that the effect of objectives receives very prominent treatment, the question of the creation of institutions and the way they change is neglected (see the critique expressed in Strang/Meyer 1993, 503ff.).

The question, therefore, is this: if it is correct that organizational structures cannot simply be changed arbitrarily into other structures, and adaptation to the environment cannot be designed according to efficiency criteria, then how do changes in organizational models come about in the first place? Or, putting it in different terms, if the strategic actions of those involved play a subordinate role in comparison to the pressure of isomorphy, how do organizations free themselves from the steel casing of the institutions and introduce variations?

The objective of this chapter is to develop an argument for why organizational models change in spite of the pressure to homogenize. We propose that organizations are increasingly using organizational structures as a marketing tool. As a result, isomorphy strategies often unfold in a way that ideas of what is "good organization" in the organization's own practice are surpassed by the organization's own innovations and variations.

In the first part (7.1), we point out not only the problems caused by the divergence of an organization's external presentation from its internal reality, but also the functions that such separation fulfills. In the second part (7.2), we show that changes in organizational structure are often undertaken for the purpose of presenting the organization to the outside world as modern and rational. A number of organizations are increasingly using organizational structure that is aligned with current management models as a product marketing tool. Part three (7.3) develops an "imitation plus" model. This is based on the assumption that the various businesses do not simply copy the ideas about rational, efficient organization that are prevalent in their environment, but introduce variations as they adjust to them. Part four is a summary and presents the argument that organizations face two disparate, often contradictory demands. The first consists of copying the ideas about rational management that are dominant in their organizational field, and thereby increasing their own legitimacy. The second requirement is to portray oneself not simply as copying organizational and product innovations undertaken elsewhere, but to initiate innovations of one's own. This polarity creates a dynamic that can lead not only to a high variability of talks within the organizations, but also to a multitude of applied organizational patterns.

7.1 The Utility of a Pleasant Appearance

Sociologist Friedrich Weltz (Weltz 2011, 67ff.) coined the incisive term "dual reality" as a means of pointing out that there are two levels of reality in organizations. One consists of designated rules, defined processes, and established structures; this is the "official reality." The other is a "practical reality" that unfolds quasi "behind the stipulated procedures." The practiced reality, which is to say, the actual modes of operation and cooperation deviate in part substantially from official work instructions, channels, organization plans, standard operating procedures, and sets of regulations.

With the catchy concept of a dual reality, Weltz—much like socio-logical neo-institutionalism and systems theoretical organizational research—touches on a sensitive issue for the fields of critical management research, the sociology of work, and industrial sociology. He points out that although the latter focuses intensively and critically on the self-descriptions of the businesses and administrations it studies, it does not recognize that practiced reality in businesses is often only loosely connected to the fashionable rationalization concepts of the day.

From this perspective, critical management research, the sociology of work, and industrial sociology appear to have a blind spot similar to the rationalistic mainstreams of management and business administration. The loudly propagated rationalization concepts are confused with operational reality, and the actually very plausible differentiation between the formal and informal aspects of an organization remains to a large degree inconsequential for empirical research. The difference between the two approaches, as seen from this point of view, is that classical management research and the science of business administration refer to the rationalization concepts in a positive sense, whereas critical management research, the sociology of work, and industrial sociology, based on their employee orientation, subject the rationalization concepts to critical questioning.

The brilliance of his observations and the acuity of his criticism notwithstanding, Friedrich Weltz has also developed a blind spot inasmuch as he treats the discrepancy between external presentation and operational reality as a problem, while overlooking its functionality. As an example, Weltz tied his observation of the discrepancy between official reality and practiced reality to a call for a greater degree of authenticity. He lamented the organizational double standard. Everybody knows, he claimed, that the other "immoral world exists," and everyone participates in it, while acting as if it weren't there. Using profitability calculations as an example, frequently everybody knows that they have nothing to do with reality, and yet they are taken at face value in internal company negotiations. In view of the huge discrepancies, the important thing is supposedly to bring the two realities closer together and thereby to promote understanding in the business (Weltz 2011, 67ff.).

A Learning Disability: Difficulties with the Dual Reality
of Businesses

Raised particularly in the field of psychological organizational research, the primary objection to the discrepancy between pious talk and actual management behavior is that the resulting cynicism has a negative effect on the organization. It is said that employees merely deride new management initiatives as the fashionable "culture of the month" and react with demotivation (see, for example, Bartlett/Ghosal 1995). It is seen as particularly problematical that a discrepancy between external presentation and operational reality could hinder learning processes. A rational and coherent presentation of the enterprise to the external world could make it difficult to bring internal problems up for discussion.

In a pioneering company, which we will call Tomolus, it was reported that, very much in keeping with the above, strong public advertising based on the firm's own group work models had led internally to the formation of circles of silence. Outside visitors at technical events were told, "We're all just great," which had the effect that the firm's own weaknesses could barely be discussed openly anymore. Because group work figured so prominently in the firm's external presentation, the associated structural problems were kept taboo until top management could no longer fail to notice the employees' growing unrest.

In another exemplary company, which we will call Acme, the employees proposed the idea that although their CEO's very high-profile external presentation would certainly produce benefits, her self-confidence was creating learning difficulties for the firm. For example, the quality assurance officer reported, "We always had a problem with that. What she presented to the external world, the things she said, didn't line up with the reality I experienced day in and day out. There was a difference, and that bothered me for a long time, because I said, 'Whatever she's saying, it's not the way things really are. So, what's that all about?'" Then, gaining insight into the underlying causes had enabled him to take a more relaxed view of the discrepancy. "So, then I talked with a psychologist, and her opinion was that beating the drum is part of the trade. Ever since then I can differentiate. She can tell the outside world anything she likes. It doesn't faze me. I know my reality, and that's it." Nevertheless, difficulties arose because the CEO actually believed what she was proclaiming. "The problem is that Ms. Meyer, the CEO, says things to the outside world, and she actually believes that's the way things are. It's a huge problem. And a lot of employees, who see her on some talk show, are saying, 'What's she talking about now? That's funny!' Sometimes she talks about the way things are here, and we don't even know about it. There are two realities."

The problem seems to be that the display side becomes progressively important for parts of management, and executives become increasingly attached to it. Internal criticism is viewed as fouling one's own nest. An effect is created which Friedrich Weltz (Weltz 2011, 169ff.) aptly describes as a "learning disability." As a consequence of the pressure to maintain the plausibility of one's own external presentations, pseudo-successes are presented as actual successes, and actual security is replaced by myths of security.

At Tomolus and Acme, the learning disability was created, in particular, because the businesses were structured in a way that is typical for mid-sized companies, and the function of the stringent and shimmering display side coincided with the function of operative management. Interestingly, many employees at these two companies were not demanding that management start reporting "honestly" about the company. Their wishes were directed instead at having the executive responsible for the firm's external presentation stay out of business operations to a greater degree. In a third company, which we will call Belzano, an employee in marketing remarked that the CEO was "a big child, a high-achiever with no love for detail," but that in a certain unit of the company business moved ahead anyway because the CEO focused exclusively on the display side. "It works, because Smith (the CEO) stays out of it." When he became involved in operative management, as he did in a different part of the company, the discrepancy between display side and company reality immediately became a problem. "If he would stay out of Cinco (the unit where he managed business operations), the outfit would run better. And if he got more involved with us (the Avda unit), then

Lord help us." At Acme, it was said that a greater distance between the display side and internal operational reality would be helpful. "The CEO would have to take a trip to an island for two years, where she couldn't reach us," the head of sales told us, "and I'm absolutely convinced things would quiet down, the business would run just as well ... we could finally get organized—by ourselves. She'd just have to go away for a year so that we can stabilize the company among ourselves, get organized." The quality assurance officer added, "She should go out and do that, she's a fantastic speaker. She should go on lecturing forever. And she fancies self-presentation a little bit, too. But here inside the company, she would have to arrange things somewhat differently."

In contrast to this conflation of display side and business operations in companies with typical midsized organization, the managers in charge of the display side in major corporations keep their distance from day-to-day organizational reality. Such distance reduces the risk that management will be held responsible on site for what is presented externally and thereby see itself forced to bring operational reality into line with the external presentation. The ability to decouple gossip, decisions, and action thematically, organizationally, and in terms of time makes it possible to absorb inconsistencies internally better than is the case in midsize companies (Brunsson 1989, 34ff./221f.).

Discussing Dual Reality on a Morally Neutral Basis

It is the merit of sociological neo-institutionalism (Meyer/Rowan 1977, 340ff.) and systems-theoretical organizational research (Kühl 2013, 138ff.) to have placed the debate over the discrepancy between display side and the organizational reality perceived by employees on morally neutral ground. This contrasts with critical management research, the sociology of work, and industrial sociology. Dual reality is no longer viewed primarily as a defect that gives rise to calls for creating greater authenticity. Instead, the focus shifts to the question: what function is fulfilled through the formation of a display side that is decoupled from internally perceived organizational reality?

Organizations face contradictory demands and norms. They must not only fulfill technical requirements and produce, say, cooking pots, software programs, and automobiles that work more or less well, but must also frequently satisfy the demands for political, legal, economic, and scientific legitimacy imposed on them through the environment. The problem now arises that the often contradictory demands from the institutional environment as a rule are not consistent with streamlined production. Calls for environmentally friendly production, shareholder demands for rationalization, or a desire to have a production method that is in step with the most current management fashion must be taken seriously, but many times present obstacles to organizing production in a streamlined, efficient manner (for a summary, see Brunsson/Olsen 1993, 8f.).

Organizations react to these contradictory demands by decoupling the internal core structures and processes, which ensure day-to-day production, from the surface structures that can be perceived from outside. Ultimately, it is this decoupling that gives organizations the freedom they require to continue operating in spite of the contradictory expectations they face. It enables them to maintain a façade that appears to be legitimate and to conform to their institutional environment, but parallel to that they can also gear their day-to-day activities to the concrete demands, thereby ensuring that production continues to function.

Nils Brunsson (Brunsson 1989; Brunsson 1993; Brunsson 2003) takes the idea of decoupling even further by speaking of "hypocrisy" or "dissimulation" as strategies that are necessary for every organization. The necessity of creating political, scientific, or legal legitimation in addition to creating products leads to discrepancies between what is expressed to the external world and internal organizational decisions and actions. An organization's actions are only loosely connected with the decisions that have been made and what is said about the organization.

The Function of the Dual Reality

The decoupling of words and actions fulfills an important function. A central function of decoupling the display side and organizational reality is that demands from the environment do not impact the organization directly. Organizations are under obligation to meet legal, political, and economic demands, yet at the same time they must ensure that ever-changing and contradictory demands to adjust do not throw their production processes into disarray.

A further important function of decoupling is that internal unrest does not immediately lead to critical inquiries from the environment. A true-to-life portrayal of organizational processes to the external world would cast doubt on the organization's legitimacy in its environment and result in critical inquiries from government agencies, the media, financial institutions, and the judiciary. All this would enter the organization in the form of uncertainty and further exacerbate internal conflict and strife. Such effects were observed when Daimler merged with Chrysler. Even though all the automobile industry experts knew that the merger would cause enormous difficulties for DaimlerChrysler, and in spite of the high degree of dissatisfaction executives expressed in surveys, the organization was able to portray the merger as a success for over two years. The corporation's CEO at the time, Jürgen Schrempp, was celebrated as the hero of the merger, and his strong media presence allowed the company to keep its internal turmoil under the surface. Even when the company's stock price collapsed—after the merger, DaimlerChrysler was at times worth less than Daimler alone beforehand—the valuation could still be portrayed as "unjustified" for some time. During the first two years, the adeptly managed discrepancy between display side and the bitter reality of the merger was helpful for the organization, because a public debate over the damage the merger had done would have hampered the process of merging internally. It was only when the CEO was replaced that employees could speak out about the problems associated with the merger, and the deal was ultimately cancelled.

The third important function of the decoupling is that it affords a certain freedom of thought, particularly for management. Since neither the environment nor the employees can legally demand authenticity, management is required to be mindful of what it says only to a limited degree. It can formulate portrayals of the organization, perceptions, thoughts, and ideas without considering whether they correspond to reality. Acme, Inc. particularly commended itself for its policy of promoting women; it participated actively in the "Total-E-Quality" campaign. By disconnecting from operational reality, management was able to propagate Acme as exemplary in the field of the advancement of women. Thus, filling management jobs exclusively with women, family-friendly working hours, and special programs for the advancement of women could arise as ideas and even be included in the organization's self-description. Internally, however, the topic of women in the company was discussed very much in terms of high staff turnover. A number of employees mentioned "strategic pregnancies" as one of the most effective means of escaping pressure in the company. The CEO, who was a woman, discussed this internally under the heading of a "remasculinization" of the firm. "We're going to have more men now, and I mean right away." "Bookkeeping is the most pregnancy-prone department. Six of them in the last several years, and I'm really fed up with it now. I said I was going to find somebody, a man, so we found Frank Meyer. And I'm going to hire another one, a man." "Now I don't know whether I'll hire three or four men—but they have to be people who are committed to making 100 million with this company, and not be simultaneously flirting with how much family time they can get." Decoupling discourse about actual hiring policies repeatedly allowed management to generate new ideas about promoting women, and even set national initiatives in motion, without allowing too much distraction by internal "needs."

7.2 Organizational Structure as a Marketing Tool

Apparently, many organizational researchers are observing that the discrepancy between down stage and backstage is growing. The formal structure of organizations is being shaped less and less through the demands of competition or efficiency, and increasingly through environmental expectations. Nils Brunsson (Brunsson 1989), for example, suspects that organizations cannot respond unequivocally and consistently to the contradictory expectations of their ever more diverse environments, and are therefore progressively decoupling technical and institutional dimensions using hypocrisy and dissimulation.

The decoupling of mythical rationality façades from actual internal behavior is often seen in relationship to the development of organizations in modern society. As an example, Klaus Türk (Türk 1995, 334) raises the question of whether Max Weber's supposition of rationality does not require modification to the effect that in Western societies the demonstration of rationality has become more important than rationality itself. In a society where the rationality paradigm is dominant, organizations are obliged to erect ceremonial, ritual-supported façades of rational procedures in order to create internal maneuvering room.

The Reasons behind the Increasing Importance of a Dual Reality

One of the reasons for the construction of rationality façades may be seen in the dependency of businesses on external but also internal (organizational) capital markets. Holding companies and banks will often approve investments only if a business conforms to relevant ideas of rational organization. Companies that are searching for capital must create the impression that the investment will allow them to adopt a value-adding strategy that will pay off financially, but also corresponds to cutting-edge management ideas. At Tomolus, for example, the holding company tied the approval of investments to the company abandoning a form of production and assembly that was strongly based on the division of labor, and introducing more group-oriented production methods. Management was able to use the new production and assembly strategy, which was widely discussed in public, to secure considerable investments in new machinery and thereby survive a dry spell. Formulating the situation more pointedly: market-listed companies depend on being traded on the capital market at a high valuation so that when they increase capital they are able to raise as substantial an amount as possible, and thereby protect themselves from hostile takeovers. Market value is also driven higher by the "fantasy" the company creates in investors. This fantasy is fueled less by a realistic description of the business's internal operations than by its rationality façade.

A second reason for the construction of rationality façades is that large companies are increasingly pressuring their suppliers to adopt a "modern" structure that suits the major buyer. Sociologist W. Richard Scott (Scott 1981) pointed out that many organizations do not receive their main impetus to create project-oriented management structures from internal sources—as a rational response to the requirements of the flow of information, so to speak—but from the outside. As an example, the US Department of Defense was already demanding that its contractors introduce project structures in the 1950s. The Department hoped this would allow it to deal with a single contact person in each company, as opposed to being passed from one contact to the next as before.

The third reason for the construction of rationality façades lies in the increasing mobility of high level executives both within and between companies. Because of this, they associate themselves with success stories in their own organizations. Managers use a successful divisionalization strategy, the introduction of a group work model, or a successful SAP project when they apply for other positions. Thus, they are not so much interested in describing projects the way they actually unfolded, but rather in linking themselves with the myths of the organization.

The three reasons cited—the importance of the capital market, dependence on important customers, and increased executive mobility—explain why creating legitimacy is gaining importance for organizations, and also why the discrepancy between the "different" realities appears to be growing. Yet there is a further reason that might explain the expanding discrepancy between down stage and backstage, namely, the necessity of using one's own structure as an advertisement.

Organizational Structure as a Marketing Tool

Classical management theory states that products and services are in demand because of their specific qualities. According to this idea, the customer is interested solely in the quality of the end product and is by and large indifferent to the production process. As long as the product fulfills its purpose, it is supposedly unimportant for the customer whether it was made and assembled on a conveyor belt, through group work, by networked independent contractors, or supplier companies.

Contrary to this assumption, in a market environment where products and services appear to be becoming ever more similar and long-term customer relationships are gaining importance, there is still a tendency for businesses to use their own organizational structures for advertising purposes. Sociologist Marshall Meyer (Meyer 1979, 494ff.) referred to this advertising strategy as "signaling." Originally, the concept of signaling referred to the jobseeker strategy of using one's formal education as a signal to employers. Employers cannot be sure how an employee will behave in the workplace. In order to evaluate employees, they therefore resort to signals such as the jobseekers' presentation, their career to date, or their education. In turn, as employees engineer their résumés they address this insecurity factor by not selecting their education and training on the basis of technical considerations alone, but also from the perspective of whether they will be sending the "right signals" to potential employers (Spence 1974, 3ff.).

Organizations engage in similar strategies. By creating new positions, flattening hierarchies, introducing group projects, or instituting new regulations, they signal that they are serious about their plans. Structural changes send stronger signals than mere window dressing in the form of speeches by the CEO and PR campaigns, because structural change requires significant investment, while speeches and PR are relatively cheap. This is why the public attaches so little value to them. To give an example, transitioning from a functionally organized business to a profit center structure has a stronger signaling effect than simply announcing that one will soon be paying closer attention to the firm's profitability. Setting up a specific department for environmental protection has a greater internal and external impact than repeatedly raising the subject in speeches by top executives.

With the concept of signaling, Marshall Meyer takes his thesis even further, that changes in organizational structures can make sense irrespective of whether or not they offer an efficiency advantage in the value-adding core. The question of changing organizational structures is quasi decoupled from considerations of direct gains in internal usefulness and viewed more strongly under the aspect of their internal and external signaling effect.

The strategy of no longer advertising through products alone, but increasingly also with one's own value-adding processes, can be found almost ideal typically in consulting firms. Companies such as Boston Consulting Group or McKinsey do not promote their services exclusively through print advertising, brochures, or books; instead, they present their own internal processes and their facilities as reference objects to their clients—such as cutting edge office space where consultants work at a different desk every day—to show that the company has taken the principles of modern office management to heart. The efficiency of internal knowledge management is presented to the client as a sales point for purchasing the firm's consulting services. The agency re-engineers its own consulting organization, thereby turning it into a reference project for clients from industry and trade.

Yet the same strategy can also be observed in companies in the more classical branches of industry and commerce. Here, too, we notice that reorganization measures are apparently not always initiated because of certain problems in the value creation process. The priority is often the "production" of a modern image instead. At Belzano, employees pointed out that the various reorganization measures such as CIP, kaizen, or the Japan Diet were initiated because they had enabled other midsized firms to win business contests. As an example, the Japan Diet was put in place after the winner of the "Factory of the Year Award" told the CEO at Belzano, "Buy this book, do exactly what I did, and in three years you'll be 'Factory of the Year.'"

At Tomolus, certain organizational measures were tackled only because customers in the automobile industry demanded the introduction of new forms of work organization. Under pressure from its customers, the company pushed through ISO 9001 certification, an ecological audit, and a range of customer-specific quality audits by adjusting its structure in ways that would allow it to pass the audits as successfully as possible.

The development in one of the holding companies was particularly interesting. It owned a loss-making and chaotically organized business unit named Cinco that was very much geared to the retail trade. Any time the company or the CEO gained public exposure, it had a direct beneficial effect on marketing. Meanwhile, an older and highly profitable business unit called Avda was exclusively geared to wholesale. Due to Cinco's strong dependence on the retail trade, organizational changes were introduced in the entire holding company so that it could project the image of a model company.

Advertising with one's own organizational structure is an indication that the homogenization tendencies of organizations are coming up against their limits. If it is correct that organizations are becoming increasingly similar in structure, then conforming to a model would no longer offer a competitive advantage. In this sense, conforming to one of the current management models would amount to a hygiene factor: one could not dispense with it, but it would also not represent any particular asset. In contradistinction to this assumption, my goal in the following is to use the above considerations on organizational structure as a marketing tool to explain the change in models of modern organizations.

7.3 Imitation Plus, Or, How Do New Forms of Organization Arise?

In organizational research, there are three standard explanations for why, in spite of the isomorphic pressure on organizations, changes occur in the models of modern organizational design. The first explanation is based on the concept of the institutional entrepreneur. Paul J.

DiMaggio (DiMaggio 1988, 14) uses this to describe players who strive to ensure the creation of new organizational concepts. Professions, lobbying organizations, and social movements endeavor to establish ideas such as "working efficiently," "humane politics," or "sustainable business" to which other players must then nod, at least in their public remarks. Depending on how strongly such "institutional projects" can be linked to existing concepts of rationality, the undertakings prove to be more or less elaborate. The classical example of this institutional entrepreneurism are consulting firms. They invest a great amount of energy in establishing ideas of "good management" which subsequently enable them to sell their consulting services.

The second explanation for changes in organizational models is based on the observation that social norms often contradict one another. As a result, organizations are forced to deviate from the norms in the pursuit of their day-to-day activities. Since it is impossible to fulfill all the norms at the same time, it becomes necessary for organizations to distance themselves from some norms and decouple their legitimation structures from their internal processes. The concept of decoupling draws attention to the fact that organizations in the same field are indeed similar in formal structure, but that in actual practice substantial differences arise. From this perspective, organizational models change in such a way that actual practice can distinguish itself in the area that is protected by rationality façades and, if it proves its worth, is integrated as an element of the display side.

The third explanation derives from the observation that the application of rules leads to variations of the rules. Even though there may be generally accepted ideas about what efficiency and effectiveness entail, the ideas must always be transferred to the circumstances of a specific organization. As the transfer takes place, the rules and programs that have been deemed sufficient and effective are adjusted, changed, and varied. It has been shown in examples of the introduction of Japanese quality circles in the USA (Strang 1997), the spread of a Japanese Buddhist movement in the USA (Snow 1993), and the diffusion of the notion of hostile takeovers (Hirsch 1986) that innovations are often the outcome of suboptimal attempts at imitating others. The variations then give rise to new institutionalizations that assert themselves through an evolutionary process.

It is possible to distinguish two directions for explaining the emergence of organizational models. The first is based on interested, active players outside of organizations who are undertaking efforts to create new institutional expectations. The second understands changes as (undesired) side effects of adaptation processes. Both directions of explanation are inclined to view as rather low an organization's chances of actively influencing the adaptation and imitation process. Yet in my view, a further point is even more important.

More Than Just Copying

My theory is that ideas of rational, efficient organization are not simply copied, and variations on them do not arise merely as undesired side effects. Rather, when adjustments to prevailing ideas of rational organization are made, processes of conscious adaptation also occur. This adaptation is not geared exclusively to making notions of "good management" practicable for one's own value creation processes; the adaptation processes are organized in such a way that an attempt is made to exceed the notions of good management, rational organization, and innovative structure. Organizations do not increase their legitimacy by merely copying ideas of rational organization, but by adding contributions of their own. Thus, imitation does not take place in the form of simply copying the ideas of rational management. During the copying process, members of the organization consider which new aspects they could use to supplement the concepts that are currently *en vogue*. The model is one of "imitation plus."

The tendency to adopt the "imitation plus" model can be observed almost ideal typically in consulting firms. They enrich current management fashions with concepts, ideas, and terminologies of their own in the hope of differentiating themselves from their competitors. Using the example of "business process reengineering," the dominant reorganization strategy in the mid-1990s, we can easily show the way different consulting firms associated themselves with this concept and gave it their own twist (Micklethwait/Wooldridge 1996). As an illustration, the consulting firm of Arthur D. Little modified the heavy IT emphasis of the reengineering concept and introduced it as the "high-performance business model." Gemini Consulting Services called its reengineering concept "business transformation," placing its own emphasis on the area of process design.

Research in organizational science informs us that industrial, commercial, and service companies—and not only consulting firms—must also present themselves as unique. Philip Selznick (Selznick 1957, 139), for example, argues that in order to survive it is essential for an organization to emphasize its unique features and convey the impression that it operates in a way that other businesses do not achieve. Organizations compete for the attention of other organizations and attempt to stand out through permanent innovation.

It is reasonable to suspect that it is enough for organizations to display their innovations merely in their external presentations, while leaving their formal side, not to mention their informal side, untroubled by them. But the more organizations spruce up their display sides, the more they are subject to the general suspicion that they are merely repeating empty phrases, and that their proclamations will bear no fruit. For this reason, in many cases organizations cannot limit themselves to talk alone.

As an example, Belzano participated in 30 business competitions annually. It employed a person whose primary responsibility was to coordinate the company's participation in the various contests. As the CEO put it, "Here at Belzano, we have the will to change and to win. After all, we enter almost 30 competitions every year—always searching for new benchmarks. Where do my colleagues stand? Where do I stand?" It was remarkable that Belzano's strategy for winning the competitions did not consist solely of following in the footsteps of the best practice business, but rather in deftly combining different management fashions, further developing management tools, or using particularly peppy concepts to portray itself as a company that was actually driving the current management discussion forward. As an example, the company advertised that it had integrated kaizen, CIP, a company suggestion system, and the Japan Diet into a comprehensive quality management system. Automotive supplier Tomolus emphasized that it had taken all of the important management concepts into account: lean management, simultaneous engineering, kanban, benchmarking, total quality management, total productivity maintenance, group work, product clinics, management by objectives, success-based compensation systems, and the learning organization approach. The CEO publicly announced, "You won't find anything that we're not already doing." But here as well, the company was attempting to signal its customers, who were very sensitive to current management fashions, that it was independently developing those concepts further. For example, Tomolus advertised that it had not only applied group work to the value-adding production and assembly processes, but that all levels of the company were organized in groups, right up to the top echelons.

At Acme, particular emphasis was placed on policies for the advancement of women. The company coined the term "leading ladies" to emphasize that it, contrary to other midsized firms, had clear guidelines to put women in management positions. It stressed that it could also imagine half-day positions for managers, which would enable this group of people to combine work and family. Easily verifiable from the outside—what is the percentage of women in leadership positions?—this personnel policy was proclaimed as one of the company's unique features, and utilized both to position itself in the employment market and for purposes of public perception.

The innovation initially takes place on the organization's display side, downstage, so to speak, but particularly when current management concepts are adopted (and exceeded) there is pressure that innovations must also be visible in actual operations. This does not eliminate the discrepancy between an attractive downstage and a significantly more flawed and inconsistent backstage. Organizations appear significantly more stringent in their display side than they are in the eyes of their employees. The decisive factor, however, is that the strategies of surpassing, in the sense of "imitation plus," are not just window dressing, but that presentation to the environment is also viewed as a motor for internal reorganization processes.

The Institutionalization of Model Innovation

The "imitation plus" strategy profits from the existence of two processes. One is that management concepts are quick to lose their distinctive fashionability. They are subject to the problem of satiation, a problem which makes it important for organizations not to present themselves as late comers, but to supplement management concepts with angles of their own. The other process is related to the mega-myth of rationality. One aspect of rationality is that it is always possible to act even more rationally. As a result, there are always opportunities for businesses to "go one better."

Organizations whose business policies simply copy a partner company or competitor and bring a "me-too product" to market create a need to explain themselves. This becomes apparent when we look at the current management discussion. Reinhard Sprenger (Sprenger 1997, 146) laments managers' tendency to "flatten their noses against the windows of their best practice competitors." According to Sprenger, "Those who walk in the footsteps of others, don't make any impressions of their own." In a similar vein, philosopher Peter Sloterdijk remarks, "You can't create uniqueness on a copy machine."

7.4 Paradoxical Demands

Organizations face two different and often contradictory demands. The first is that they copy the ideas of rational management that dominate their organizational field and thereby increase their own legitimacy. The second is that they must not present themselves as merely copying organizational and product innovations created elsewhere, but also as initiating innovations of their own.

Organizations view the "imitation plus" model presented above as a promising strategy for meeting the partially contradictory demands of their environment. By copying currently dominant management models in this manner, they address the expectation of rational, modern management. Yet they also fulfill the demand for innovation by supplementing their organizational model with their own competencies and portraying these as organizational innovations to their customers, suppliers, and competitors.

8.
Beyond a Restricted Instrumental-Rational Understanding of Organizations

"Perfect order would be the ruin
of all progress and enjoyment."
Robert Musil

The main advantage of understanding the paradoxes and dilemmas of organizations more deeply lies in gaining access to their contingency. An organization consists of nothing other than the decisions it repeatedly makes in its day-to-day processes, and not much more. Niklas Luhmann (Luhmann 2003) expresses this opinion in a statement that appears esoteric at first sight, namely, that organizations are systems that consist of decisions and produce the decisions of which they consist by themselves, through the very decisions of which they consist.

The reason this process functions is because organizations do not continually bear in mind the contingency of their own decisions, but repeatedly introduce shortcuts: previous decisions are viewed as so self-evident that no consideration is given, say, to whether technical processes are justified or whether a market orientation is logical. The assumption is that market changes have occurred that allow only one course of action, such as greater technologization, job cuts, or innovation.

The paradox of the decision is that each decision has the effect of either making subsequent decisions possible or preventing them (Luhmann 1993, 298f.). Irrespective of whether the decisions are structural and stipulate new regulations, new communication channels, and personnel changes, or are simply mini-decisions that clarify questions arising over the short-term, organizations have no choice but to base their current decisions on previous ones, thereby screening out the limitations entailed in calculating the ones that were made before.

8.1 It Is Impossible to Continuously Consider Paradoxes and Dilemmas

Organizations cannot constantly bear in mind all of their paradoxes and dilemmas. The problem is that constantly making paradoxes and dilemmas the subject of discussion would construct a complex and diverse view of the political, economical, scientific, and cultural environment, but that would make it increasingly difficult for them to demarcate themselves in relationship to their surroundings. Unbridled development of paradoxes and dilemmas would generate internal complexity that would indeed do justice to the complexity of the environment, but would ultimately make it impossible for the organization to achieve internal stability.

There is no meta-rule for when organizations should elaborate paradoxes in their self-portrayals and when they should screen them out. This has the effect that every organization swings from one decision to the next and does not realize until afterward whether or not all the decisions contribute to its further existence. Every simplification that ignores paradoxes is vulnerable to disruptions that point to circumstances not taken into account (Luhmann 2000, 123ff.). Just as managers can draw attention to missed opportunities, shareholders can point to competitive situations that have not been addressed, unions to business errors, and consultants to changing ideas on the "one best way." Nevertheless—and this is what makes the difference—the chances of being taken seriously, and not merely dismissed as static, vary.

An understanding of organizations that goes beyond instrumental-rational concepts is not tantamount to "anything goes." On the contrary, since organizations can ultimately build only on their previous decisions, they are committed to decision-making corridors and developmental paths. This commitment has the effect that paradoxes and dilemmas repeatedly manifest, to which the organization must react with new deliberations, discussions, and decisions. This process always results in problems because organizations can never know whether or not they will continue to exist with their decision chains. Since they can only perceive a limited spectrum of their environment, and the future remains necessarily unclear, organizations can never be certain whether their decisions are right. Market observations, field research, observing competitors, internal evaluation processes, and employee surveys can provide a sense of security. Ultimately, however, such actions always result in surrogate security that is produced by the organization itself with all of its limited perceptual abilities (Luhmann 2005). Thus, organizations face a dilemma. They can decide in favor of a cultivated illusion by persuading themselves that they have acted rationally in the best sense of the word. Or they can permit cultivated incongruence and hope that the elaboration of paradoxes, dilemmas, and contradictions will develop into a more complex worldview, albeit one that also has a tendency to block decisions.

8.2 The Benefit of the Sisyphean Task

It may make sense not to lose faith in one's ability to reach the summit and, like Sisyphus, to keep rolling the boulder up the hill. Perhaps the constant striving for an optimal organizational structure is the very function of management itself. If businesses, government agencies, or hospitals functioned like clockwork, or a machine, there would be no reason to employ people to manage uncertainty. If one succeeded in depositing the boulder at the peak, management would render itself superfluous.

In brief, a manager's job description boils down to the idea of undertaking a Sisyphean task. In the thoroughly organized, value-adding processes of assembly line, call center, and administrative organizations, the dilemma for employees is that they jeopardize their own jobs through organizational optimizations. Managers, on the other hand, can depend on an organization continually providing surprising new contradictions, side effects, and paradoxes to occupy them. Managers will only need to worry about justifying their existence when the impression arises that their work no longer has the character of a Sisyphean task, and that everything is running like clockwork.

Methodological Epilogue

The material I use for my organizational scientific books draws on three sources: my own research projects, in which I pursue specific questions; consulting projects, which generate interesting insights into organizations quasi as byproducts; and accounts of specific organizations that have been prepared by other consultants, executives, or scientists.

In analyzing the organizations mentioned in this book, I resorted to a method I used in my book *When the Monkeys Run the Zoo: The Pitfalls of Flat Hierarchies* and subsequently developed further in various research projects. It consists of focusing on organizations that pioneered decentralization. I define pioneering organizations as those that drew attention to themselves through the introduction of organizational features that are considered modern (decentralization, dehierarchization, the dismantling of functional division of labor) and stood as models for organizations in the same field.

The case analysis of organizations that pioneered decentralization stands in contrast to the methodologies of both contingency theory-oriented organizational research and of industrial psychology, with its interest in comprehensive trends. These disciplines generally refer to "typical" businesses, governmental agencies, hospitals, or universities, and strive to match as many variables as possible. Contrary to this method, my objective is not primarily to develop an empirically documented thesis based on extensive samples. Instead, the examination of pioneering organizations serves to develop considerations and to illustrate a theoretically supported argumentation.

The problem in studying organizations in general, and pioneering ones in particular, is that the initial accounts given by discussion partners merely portray the organization's display side. The dominant tenor of management is that clear goals are set, instructions are given, deviations are measured, and re-adjustments are made. What managers tell researchers is often geared to the lists of objectives, visions, and plans that are circulating in the business.

As an outsider, one risks confusing the organization's display side with its formal or informal aspects. While constructing an external presentation has a function for an organization, it presents a limited view. The façade often presents intentions which, as Nils Brunsson (Brunsson 1989, 231ff.) points out, often do not materialize. The cause-and-effect chains portrayed on the display side are often much different from those found in day-to-day operations. The in part mythical portrayal of the relationships between certain causes and effects fulfill an important function, but they are not a realistic reflection of what goes on in the firm. Reconstructing the façades of pioneering organizations is important; equally pivotal, however, are the accounts of day-to-day operational reality given by employees.

For this reason, I have tried as much as possible to work with three special methodological features in order to achieve this level of description. First, a multi-point analysis was conducted in each of the businesses. Visiting the companies a number of times allowed us to detect inconsistencies in descriptions. Second, a mixture of various methods from empirical social research was used. Particularly, the combination of one-on-one interviews, group discussions, and observation made it possible to identify discrepancies in self-descriptions. Third, in some of the one-on-one interviews and the group discussions the interviewers changed their style half way through. When those surveyed showed strong attachment to the firm's downstage metaphors, after somewhat collaborative prompting and questioning at the beginning, we switched to a confrontational style. The individual or group was explicitly challenged with the (possible) discrepancy and asked to provide an explanation. Some of the discussion partners reacted defensively to this change in style, but in other situations the conversation shifted direction and participants provided accounts that no longer matched up with the display side presentations.

When using this methodological approach, the object is not to discredit the rational façades presented in the interviews through an alleged "actual reality." Rather, working out the discrepancy between organizational downstage and backstage is a necessary step for grasping the adaptation, construction, and further development of models as an autonomous process that is only loosely coupled with the reality of day-to-day operations. Only then does it become possible to elaborate how organizations adjust to models and further develop them.

Bibliography

Ackroyd, Stephen, Gibson Burrell, Michael Hughes, and Alan Whitaker. 1988. "The Japanisation of British Industry?" *Industrial Relations Journal*, no. 19: 11–23.

Argyris, Chris. 1985. *Strategy, Change and Defensive Routines*. London: Pitman.

Baecker, Dirk. 1999. *Organisation als System*. Frankfurt a.M.: Suhrkamp.

Baker, Wayne E. 1990. "Market Networks and Corporate Behavior." *American Journal of Sociology*, no. 96: 589–625.

Barnard, Chester I. 1938. *The Functions of the Executive*. Cambridge: Harvard University Press.

Bartlett, Christopher, and Sumantra Ghoshal. 1995. "Changing the Role of Top Management: Beyond Systems to People." *Harvard Business Review* 73, no. 3: 132–142.

Beekun, Rafik I. 1989. "Assessing the Effectiveness of Sociotechnical Interventions: Antidote or Fad?" *Human Relations*, no. 42: 877–897.

Bendell, Tony. 2006. "A Review and Comparison of Six Sigma and the Lean Organisations." *The TQM Magazine*, no. 18: 255–262.

Berger, Ulrike. 1984. *Wachstum und Rationalisierung der industriellen Dienstleistungsarbeit*. Frankfurt a.M./New York: Campus.

Berger, Ulrike. 1988. "Rationalität, Macht und Mythen." In *Mikropolitik Rationalität, Macht und Spiele in Organisationen*, edited by Willi Küpper, and Günther Ortmann,115–130. Opladen: WDV.

Braverman, Harry. 1974. *Labor and Monopoly Capital: The Degradation of Work in the Twentieth Century*. New York/London: Monthly Review Press.

Brunsson, Nils. 1989. *The Organization of Hypocrisy: Talk, Decisions and Actions in Organizations*. Chichester: Wiley.

Brunsson, Nils. 1993. "The Necessary Hypocrisy." *International Executive*, no. 35: 1–9.

Brunsson, Nils. 2003. "Organized Hypocrisy." In *The Northern Lights: Organization Theory in Scandinavia*, edited by Barbara Czarniawska, and Guje Sevón, 201–222. Copenhagen/Malmö/Oslo: Copenhagen Business School Press.

Brunsson, Nils, and Johan P. Olsen. 1993. *The Reforming Organization*. London/NewYork: Routledge.

Burawoy, Michael. 1979. *Manufacturing Consent*. Chicago/London: The University of Chicago Press.

Castoriadis, Cornelius. 1998. *The Imaginary Institution of Society*. Cambridge, Mass: MIT Press.

Child, John, Hans-Dieter Ganter, and Alfred Kieser. 1987. "Technological Innovation and Organizational Conservatism." In *New Technology as Organizational Innovation: The Development and Diffusion of Microelectronics*, edited by Johannes M. Pennings, and Arend Buitendam, 87–115. Cambridge: Ballinger.

Coase, Ronald H. 1937. "The Nature of the Firm." *Economica*, no. 17: 386–405.

Commons, John R. 1924. *Legal Foundations of Capitalism*. NewYork: Macmillan.

Crozier, Michel. 1964. *The Bureaucratic Phenomenon*. London: Tavistock.

Crozier, Michel, and Erhard Friedberg. 1977. *L'acteur et le système*. Paris: Seuil.

Cyert, Richard M., and James G. March. 1963. *A Behavioral Theory of the Firm*. Englewood Cliffs: Prentice-Hall.

David, Paul A. 1985. "Clio and the Economics of QWERTY." *The American Economic Review*, no. 75: 332–337.

David, Paul A. 1986. "Understanding the Economics of QWERTY: The Necessity of History." In *Economic History and the Modern Economist*, edited by William N. Parker, 30–49. Oxford: Blackwell.

Deal, Terrence E., and Allan A. Kennedy. 1982. *Corporate Cultures: The Rites and Rituals of Corporate Life*. Reading: Addison-Wesley.

DiMaggio, Paul J. 1988. "Interest and Agency in Institutional Theory." In *Institutional Patterns and Organizations: Culture and Environment*, edited by Lynne G. Zucker, 3–21. Cambridge: Ballinger.

DiMaggio, Paul J., and Walter W. Powell. 1983. "The Iron Cage Revisited: Institutional Isomorphism and Collective Rationality in Organizational Fields." *American Sociological Review*, no. 48: 147–160.

Edwards, Richard C. 1979. *Contested Terrain*. New York: Basic Books.

Farson, Richard. 1997. *Management of the Absurd: Paradoxes in Leadership*. New York: Touchstone.

Friedberg, Erhard. 1993. *Le Pouvoir et la Règle: Dynamiques de l'Actionorganisée*. Paris: Seuil.

Gouldner, Alvin W. 1954. *Patterns of Industrial Bureaucracy*. New York: Free Press.

Grabher, Gernot. 1993. "The Weakness of Strong Ties: The Lock-in of Regional Development in the Ruhr Area." In *The Embedded Firm: On the Socioeconomics of Industrial Networks*, edited by Gernot Grabher, 255–277. London/New York: Routledge.

Gutenberg, Erich. 1983. *Grundlagen der Betriebswirtschaftslehre: Die Produktion*, 24th ed. Berlin: Springer.

Hammer, Michael, and James Champy. 1993. *Reengineering the Corporation: A Manifesto for Business Revolution*. New York: HarperBusiness.

Hannan, Michael T., and John Freeman. 1977. "The Population Ecology of Organizations." *American Journal of Sociology*, no. 82: 929–964.

Hedberg, Bo. 1981. "How Organizations Learn and Unlearn." In *Handbook of Organizational Design*, edited by Paul C. Nystrom, and William H. Starbuck, 3–27. Oxford: Oxford University Press.

Hirsch, Paul M. 1986. "From Ambushes to Golden Parachutes: Corporate Takeovers as an Instance of Cultural Framing and Institutional Integration." *American Journal of Sociology*, no. 91: 800–837.

Hodgson, Damian E. 2004. "Project Work: The Legacy of Bureaucratic Control in the Post-Bureaucratic Organization." *Organization*, no. 11: 81–100.

Hodgson, Damian E., and Louise Briand. 2013. "Controlling the Uncontrollable: >Agile< Teams and Illusions of Autonomy in Creative Work." *Work, Employment & Society*, no. 27: 308–325.

Imai, Masaaki. 1986. *Kaizen (Ky'zen), the Key to Japan's Competitive Success*. New York: Random House.

Juran, Josef M. 1991. *Handbuch der Qualitätsplanung*, 3rd ed. Landsberg am Lech: Moderne Industrie.

Kieser, Alfred. 1994. "Fremdorganisation, Selbstorganisation und evolutionäres Management." *Zeitschrift für betriebswirtschaftliche Forschung*, no. 46: 199–228.

Koch, Rainer. 1993. "Entscheidungsstile und Entscheidungsverhalten von Führungskräften öffentlicher Verwaltungen." *Verwaltung und Fortbildung*, no. 21: 179–197.

Kötter, Wolfgang, and Gerd Kullmann. 1996. "Arbeitsorganisation im Jahr 2000." *STZ*, no. 5: 41–43.

Kühl, Stefan. 2013. *Organizations: A Systems Approach*. Surrey: Gower Publishing.

Laloux, Frederic. 2014. *Reinventing Organizations: A Guide to Creating Organizations Inspired by the Next Stage of Human Consciousness*. Brussels: Nelson Parker.

Lattmann, Charles. 1972. *Das norwegische Modell der selbstgesteuerten Arbeitsgruppe: Beitrag zur Verwirklichung der Mitbestimmung am Arbeitsplatz*. Bern: Paul Haupt.

Legge, Karen. 2002. "On Knowledge, Business Consultants and the Selling of TQM." In *Critical Consulting: New Perspectives on the Management Advice Industry*, edited by Timothy Clark, and Robin Fincham, 74–92. Oxford/Malden: Blackwell.

Likert, Rensis. 1961. *New Patterns of Management*. New York: McGraw-Hill.

Luhmann, Niklas. 1964. *Funktionen und Folgen formaler Organisation*. Berlin: Duncker & Humblot.

Luhmann, Niklas. 1969. *Legitimation durch Verfahren*. Neuwied/Berlin: Luchterhand.

Luhmann, Niklas. 1971. *Politische Planung: Aufsätze zur Soziologie von Politik und Verwaltung*. Opladen: WDV.

Luhmann, Niklas. 1973. *Zweckbegriff und Systemrationalität: Über die Funktion von Zwecken in sozialen Systemen*. Frankfurt a.M.: Suhrkamp.

Luhmann, Niklas. 1993. "Die Paradoxie des Entscheidens." *Verwaltungsarchiv*, no. 84: 287–310.

Luhmann, Niklas. 1995. *Funktionen und Folgen formaler Organisation*, 4th ed. Berlin: Duncker & Humblot.

Luhmann, Niklas. 1997. *Die Gesellschaft der Gesellschaft*. Frankfurt a.m.: Suhrkamp.

Luhmann, Niklas. 2000. *Organisation und Entscheidung*. Opladen: WDV.

Luhmann, Niklas. 2003. "Organization." In *Autopoietic Organization Theory: Drawing on NiklasLuhmann's Social Systems Perspective*, edited by Tore Bakken, and Tor Hernes, 31–52. Copenhagen: Copenhagen Business School Press.

Luhmann, Niklas. 2005. "Communication Barriers in Management Consulting." In *Niklas Luhmann and Organization Studies*, edited by Kai Helge Becker, and David Seidl, 351–364. Philadelphia/Amsterdam: John Benjamins.

March, James G. 1962. "The Business Firm as a Political Coalition." *The Journal of Politics*, no. 24: 662–678.

March, James G. 1994. *A Primer on Decision Making: How Decisions Happen*. New York: Free Press.

March, James G., and Herbert A. Simon. 1958. *Organizations*. New York: John Wiley.

McSweeney, Brendan. 2006. "Are We Living in a Post-Bureaucratic Epoch?" *Journal of Organizational Change Management*, no. 19: 22–37.

Mechanic, David. 1962. "Sources of Power of Lower Participants in Complex Organizations." *Administrative Science Quarterly*, no. 7: 349–364.

Meyer, Marshall W. 1979. "Organizational Structure as Signaling." *Pacific Sociological Review*, no. 22: 481–500.

Meyer, John W., and Brian Rowan. 1977. "Institutionalized Organizations: Formal Structure as Myth and Ceremony." *American Journal of Sociology*, no. 83: 340–363.

Meyer, Marshall W., and Lynne Zucker. 1989. *Permanently Failing Organizations*. London: Sage.

Micklethwait, John, and Adrian Wooldridge. 1996. *The Witch Doctors: Making Sense of the Management Gurus*. London: William Heinemann.

Midler, Christophe. 1986. "La Logiques de la Mode Managériale." *Gérer et Comprendre*, no. 3: 74–85.

Mintzberg, Henry. 1979. *The Structuring of Organizations: A Synthesis of the Research*. Englewood Cliffs: Prentice-Hall.

Mintzberg, Henry, Bruce Ahlstrand, and Joseph Lampel. 2009. *Strategy Safari: The Complete Guide through the Wilds of Strategic Management*. Harlow, UK: FT Prentice Hall.

Moullet, Michel. 1983. *La Concurrence Organisée*. Paris: PhD diss., IEP Paris.

Ortmann, Günther. 1994. "Lean: Zur rekursiven Stabilisierung von Kooperation." In *Managementforschung 4*, edited by Georg Schreyögg, and Peter Conrad, 143–184. Berlin/New York: de Gruyter.

Peters, Thomas J., and Robert Waterman. 1982. *In Search of Excellence: Lessons from America's Best-Run Companies*. New York: Harper & Row.

Polanyi, Karl. 1957. *The Great Transformation*. Boston: Beacon Press.

Quinn, Robert E. 1988. *Beyond Rational Management: Mastering the Paradoxes and Competing Demands of High Performance*. San Francisco: Jossey-Bass.

Quinn, Robert E., and Kim S. Cameron. 1988. *Paradox and Transformation: Toward a Theory of Change in Organization and Management*. Cambridge: Ballinger.

Robertson, Brian J. 2015. *Holacracy: The New Management System for a Rapidly Changing World*. New York: Holt.

Scott, W. Richard. 1981. *Organizations: Rational, Natural, and Open Systems*. Englewood Cliffs, N.J.: Prentice-Hall.

Selznick, Philip. 1957. *Leadership in Administration*. Evanston: Row Peterson.

Simon, Fritz B. 1997. *Die Kunst, nicht zu lernen: Und andere Paradoxien in Psychotherapie, Management, Politik*. Heidelberg: Carl-Auer Verlag.

Simon, Herbert A. 1965. "The Architecture of Complexity." *General Systems*, no. 10: 63–76.

Smith, Kenwyn K., and David N. Berg. 1997. *Paradoxes of Group Life: Understanding Conflict, Paralysis, and Movement in Group Dynamics*. San Francisco: Jossey-Bass.

Snow, David A. 1993. *Shakubuku: A Study of the Nichiren Shoshu Buddhist Movement in America, 1960-1975*. New York/London: Garland.

Spence, A. Michael. 1974. *Market Signaling: Informational Transfer in Hiring and Related Screening Processes*. Cambridge: Harvard University Press.

Sprenger, Reinhard K. 1997. "Mit Appetitzüglern ernährt." *Wirtschaftswoche*, no. 8.5: 146.

Starbuck, William H. 1988. "Surmounting Our Human Limitations." In *Paradox and Transformation: Toward a Theory of Change in Organization and Management*, edited by Robert E. Quinn, and Kim Cameron, 65–80. Cambridge: Ballinger.

Strang, David. 1997. "Cheap Talk: Managerial Discourse on Quality Circles as an Organizational Innovation." Paper presented at the Annual Meeting of the American Sociological Association, Toronto.

Strang, David, and John W. Meyer. 1993. "Institutional Conditions for Diffusions." *Theory and Society*, no. 22: 487–511.

Sturdy, Andrew, Christopher Wright, and Nick Wylie. 2014. "Managers as Consultants: The Hybridity and Tensions of Neo-Bureaucratic Management." *Organization*, no. 21: 1–22.

Thompson, James D. 1967. *Organizations in Action*. New York: McGraw-Hill.

Türk, Klaus. 1995. *Die Organisation der Welt: Herrschaft durch Organisation in der modernen Gesellschaft*. Opladen: WDV.

Udy, Stanley H. 1959. "Bureaucracy and Rationality in Weber's Organization Theory." *American Sociological Review*, no. 24: 791–795.

Vansina, Leopold S., and Tarsi Taillieu. 1996. "Business Process Reengineering oder soziotechnisches Systemdesign in neuen Kleidern?" In *Organisationsentwicklung und Supervision: Erfolgsfaktoren bei*

Veränderungsprozessen, edited by Gerhard Fatzer, 19–44. Köln: Edition Humanistische Psychologie.

Weber, Max. 1976. *Wirtschaft und Gesellschaft*, 5th ed. Tübingen: J.C.B. Mohr.

Weber, Wolfgang G. 1997. *Analyse von Gruppenarbeit: Kollektive Handlungsregulation in soziotechischen Systemen*. Bern: Huber.

Weick, Karl E. 1976. "Educational Organizations as Loosely Coupled Systems." *Administrative Science Quarterly*, no. 21: 1–19.

Weltz, Friedrich. 2011. *Nachhaltige Innovation: Ein industriesoziologischer Ansatz zum Wandel in Unternehmen*. Berlin: Edition Sigma.

White, Harrison C., and Robert G. Eccles. 1986. "Control via Concentration." *Sociological Forum*, no. 1: 131–157.

Wittel, Andreas. 1998. "Gruppenarbeit und Arbeitshabitus." *Zeitschrift für Soziologie*, no. 27:178–192.

Womack, James P., Daniel T. Jones, and Daniel Ross. 1990. *The Machine that Changed the World*. New York: Maxwell Macmillan International.